SMART DATING RULES FOR CHRISTIAN WOMEN

BIBLICAL WISDOM & GUIDANCE FOR LOVE & RELATIONSHIPS

SARITA A. FOXWORTH

Books by Sarita A. Foxworth

Spiritual Growth
- How to Heal a Broken Heart: Transition From Pain to Peace
- The Single Woman's Prayer Book: How to Get Answers From Heaven
- The Proverbs 31 Woman's Devotional: 31 Days To A Renewed Mind & Spirit
- How God Speaks: The Ultimate Guide to Hearing From God Clearly & Consistently
- Sarita Foxworth's Faith-Based Fasting Planner

Life's Purpose and Calling
- The Prophetic Woman: Boldly Declaring the Word of the Lord
- Find Your Purpose: The Ultimate Guide to Unveiling and Stepping Into Your God-Given Life's Purpose
- Dream Interpretation Journal: Record Holy Spirit Inspired Dreams, Visions and Prophetic Words

Love, Dating, and Relationships
- How to Prepare for Your Future Husband: Waiting, Dating & Trusting God for Your Adam
- Giving Birth to Miracles: Manifesting Supernatural Childbirth
- Smart Dating Rules for Christian Women: Biblical Wisdom & Guidance for Love, Dating & Relationships
- Book Marketing
- Attracting an Audience of Book Buyers for New Authors

To connect with Sarita or order group books and beautiful gifts for your next event visit: www.SaritaFoxworth.com

SMART DATING RULES

FOR

CHRISTIAN WOMEN

BIBLICAL WISDOM & GUIDANCE
FOR LOVE & RELATIONSHIPS

SARITA A. FOXWORTH

First Printing, 2022

ISBN: 9798405231143
Published By L & M Publishing, LLC Impublishing.co

CONTENTS

DEDICATION

This work is dedicated to my dear friend, Cozette. You are one of the most pure-hearted people I know, a beautiful woman of God who has never given up on love.

INTRODUCTION:

THE BIBLE DOESN'T TALK ABOUT DATING

After over 11 years of coaching, teaching, and mentoring women of God who desire to be married, I can tell you one thing for sure... the Bible has a lot to say about dating, love, and relationships. The Lord cares about who we give our hearts to. He cares about who we marry and have children with. God cares about every single aspect of our lives, and the person with whom we will share our life is no exception.

What I will show you within these pages is how you can seek the Word and wisdom of God to find answers and guidance to your dating, love, and relationship choices. My desire is that you live a beautiful life and have a peaceful, joyful, and blessed dating season. You can avoid wasted time, heartache, or even worse, marrying and having children with a person who is wrong for you. God wants you to be one with an amazing man of God. He makes the rules for us.

As you dive in, use various Bible translations and contextual research to help you gain a greater understanding. Be sure to spend quality time with the Father in prayer, so that he can give you personalized guidance for your specific situation. Additional resources for working with me in real life can be found in the "About the Author" section of this book.

I am praying for you. No matter when you are reading this book, know that you have been prayed for by me and I am in agreement with you for wanting God to send you an exceeding, abundant, agape, and pure love.

PART 1:

PRACTICAL, BIBLICAL, AND TRANSPARENT WISDOM

RULE #1:

SET & STICK TO YOUR STANDARDS

When it comes to living your life as a Christian woman, there are certain standards, expectations, and requirements that should be mandatory. Trusting that God will send you a man that will live his life in accordance with the standards and limitations established in the Word of God is not asking for too much.

It's unfortunate that the society we live in would have Christian women believe that certain scriptures are optional or "up for interpretation" when, in fact, these scriptures are clearly stated instructions from God for how we should live our lives and make personal decisions.

Life is easier when we allow the Word

SCAN ME

Watch this video where I discuss the top dating standards every Christian woman should have in greater detail.

of God to govern our actions. Here are some basic standards that all women of God should have in place during their dating season. These standards are all biblically based and should trump all personal feelings or philosophy brought on by human emotion or societal norms.

♡ **He must be a Christian.** Second Corinthians 6:14 lets us know that we should not be bound to those who do not share our beliefs. In other words, Christians should not date or marry non-Christians. It's impossible for a couple to be on one accord, with one vision of worshipping, serving, and glorifying God if they don't believe in the same God and that Jesus Christ is the ONLY Lord & Savior. For more about this topic, visit the Rules for Cross Denomination Dating in Part 2.

♡ **He must act like a Christian.** Ephesians 5:1-21 tells us exactly how Christians should act, in love, light, and wisdom. There are outward manifestations when the Spirit of God is present. Perfection is not required of anyone, but expecting a man to act like a Christian, an imitator of Christ as the scripture states, is not asking for too much.

♡ **He must desire marriage AND be husband material.** Ephesians 5:23-31 defines what a God-glorifying marriage looks like and feels like. As you examine the instructions given by God for how husbands are to cover and love their wives, it is clear what the Lord defines as husband material. If you are dating a man who cannot fulfill the requirements God has laid out or if he has no revelation or concept of what God requires of him once he is a husband, I recommend not giving your heart to him.

♡ **He must be single.** Unfortunately, this standard is not self-explanatory. Proverbs 6:32 and many other scriptures reveal the Lord's stance on adultery. He is vehemently against it. I have advised women who are single that if they believe the Lord has revealed a man is their future husband, yet this particular man in question is still married (including if he is "going through" a divorce), that on the contrary, God has not spoken to them. I have warned them that they should be concerned about the deception of the spirit of adultery. The Bible teaches that God is a God of order (1 Corinthians 14:40). If he sends a man to find you, that man will be in the same state as you are when he finds you, he will be single.

♡ **He must be cute in your eyes.** Proverbs 10:24 gives us a promise that our desires will be granted, simply because we are righteous. To be righteous is to be in good standing with God. Because of the blood of Jesus, we are instantly made righteous on the day of our salvation. Trust that God will give you the desire of a husband that is handsome in your eyes. Desiring a man of God that you are physically attracted to, is not asking for too much.

All other standards you have set for the type of man you want to marry will fall under Psalm 37:4. The Lord is your Abba Father. Any father wants their daughter to marry well and live a happy, blessed life. Maintaining biblical standards that are in alignment with the heart of God is wise and very possible for you, no matter how impossible it may seem.

HIGHLIGHT THIS: Your desires in a man or a relationship are God's desires for you. You are a woman of God. When you receive the free gift of salvation and are born again, your desires become God's desires (Philippians 2:13). This means you can trust that your desires are in alignment with the will of God when those desires stem from a deep-rooted, inner spiritual place. This is the location of the Holy Spirit within you, the seat of purpose, love, and peace. Let me prove this to you. Right now, close your eyes and think of the top three things you want in a husband. What came to mind? Each time I have conducted this real-time experiment with a group of 20+ women the responses were loving, kind, faithful, loyal, provider, protector, leader, spiritually strong, etc. I am sure your answers were along these lines. There is nothing demonic or ungodly about desiring a good man who provides for his family and takes care of the home. There is nothing wrong with desiring a husband that is spiritually strong and a good father. In fact, these desires for a loving marriage are in alignment with God's desires and his original purpose for marriage, found in Ephesians Chapter 5. Stop questioning yourself and give yourself permission to desire nothing but God's best for your life!

RULE #2:

BE PICKY. YOUR HEART, MIND, BODY, AND SOUL MATTER

W hen you reach a certain age or have been single for what seems to be a significant amount of time you may start to believe you are being too picky. There may also be other voices in your life that try to convince you that your standards are too high and you are being too rigid when it comes to your desires and standards. When well-meaning friends and family make these types of statements to you, you start to wonder if, in fact, you are "keeping yourself" single by having non-negotiable requirements for the man of God you are praying for.

While there is a difference between superficial and purpose-driven desires and standards, most often the type of man you are praying for does not indicate you are expecting or asking for too much. The Lord is not limited in his ability to provide for and take care of you, including your needs and desires. Remember, God is your Father. Every father wants his daughter to marry well. Every father wants his daughter to be with a man who loves her and treats her like a queen with respect and dignity. You have expectations and requirements for every other type of relationship in your life. Having a relationship with a man that could lead to a lifelong union of marriage, is one of the most important relationships you will ever have. Give yourself permission to trust God for the best relationship with an amazing man of God. There is nothing wrong with having expectations of the same high standards you hold yourself to.

The spiritual standards that you have should be non-negotiable since they are in alignment with the will of God. Not only does Ephesians Chapter 5 tell men what their role is as a kingdom husband, but the Word of God is filled with true men of God who understood how to spiritually cover, protect, provide and care for their family. The Bible also instructs us not to be unequally yoked (2 Corinthians 6:14) or in other words, date, give your heart to, or marry an unbeliever. Based on these two biblical references, it is clear that the men we get involved with should be saved and able to cover our family spiritually, leading us and our future (current) children closer to God as a result of the relationship itself. Expecting the man that God sends to be spiritually mature and a true man of valor is not being too picky.

The level of spiritual maturity you need is going to be based on exactly where you are in your walk with Christ. If you have been on a path of spiritual growth, gaining a deeper understanding and personal revelation followed by life transformation, the man that God will send will also have experienced a certain level of spiritual growth commensurate with yours. For a deeper conversation about being unequally yoked, visit the Rules for Cross Denominational Dating in Part 2.

Now, let's talk about the superficial standards and desires you may have: things like how he looks, how much money he makes, his level of education, career status, or lifestyle. Most of the women I have worked with who believe or are being told that they are being too picky, are not asking God to send them a rich male

SCAN ME

Watch a video where I answered the question: "What if he is not my type, could he be the one?"

model. They are not in faith for the CEO of a Fortune 500 company who owns a private jet and is super fine with an eight pack, perfect teeth, and skin. Sometimes these are the same women who are wondering if God wants them to be with a man who is unattractive. They wonder if God may want them to be the breadwinner in the home since they are already successful. They also consider that God might send them a man who would possibly be a new Christian or not as in tune with his purpose or spiritual calling as they are.

Think about the last relationship you were in with a man who did not meet your spiritual and natural standards. How did it work out? Most of the time you will find that even without those standards, when you were lacking in your requirements and negotiated or completely removed the non-negotiables, the relationship was not blessed. You probably ended up hurt or even regretting the relationship. Also, think about where those desires and requests to God are stemming from.

It's not unreasonable to desire a man you are attracted to. In fact, men who are whole spiritually, mentally, and emotionally will only consider marrying a woman they are physically attracted to...it's a given. Men don't wonder if their missing rib is a woman they think is ugly. The very first factor that even draws a man to a woman is physical attraction. Obviously, the attraction does not stop at the physical, but it certainly is important. Chances are, you wouldn't even want to be with a man that was not physically attracted to you, but he admired your worship of God. You want a man that thinks you're beautiful and magnetic, in addition to the fact that he loves how you serve and honor the Lord.

There are always those individuals who believe that God is not concerned with the physical attraction between a couple. They believe that God's plan and purpose are so much higher than ours, that he can't possibly expect a woman to be attracted to her husband and vice versa. When you think about who God is and understand the chemical makeup of men and women he created, including our differences and the fact that we need to have sex with only the one person we will be married to always, it only makes sense that the Lord would want each partner in a couple to be attracted to the other. Every person on this planet looks different. Every person in creation is unique. Likewise, every person likes different things about the physical makeup of another. In other words, every man doesn't like or want the same type of woman (physically speaking), nor is every woman attracted to every type of man. We each like what we like. God made us different on purpose. There is someone for everyone and we can trust that the Lord already knows what we like. He is not limited in his power to deliver a spouse of our liking by connecting us with a man we are attracted to.

When it comes to the amount of money the man of God makes, the focus should not be so much on the quantitative value of his income, but rather on his ability to provide for his family as a man. Again, when we do a full study of the Word of God, we will find that men always provided for their families. There is not a biblical example of a woman who worked in the fields while her husband was at home unemployed.

The generation we live in has allowed women to flourish in the marketplace, whether in a career field or the entrepreneurial arena. Prayerfully your future husband's success will match yours, but even if it does not, he will still be gainfully employed enough to provide for your family while you continue to enjoy the quality of life you are accustomed to. If there is too big a gap between your incomes, there will be stress and strain on the relationship. Money concerns will always be a factor or an issue. It is extremely important that you and the man you marry make, manage, invest and distribute money in a similar or same manner. The quality of life you enjoy as a single woman should be the same or rise to another level once you are married. It certainly shouldn't suffer. How is God glorified in you having to downgrade your lifestyle or take care of a man AND your children as a woman?

A real-life example I know is a prominent woman who generates millions of dollars as a serial entrepreneur. When she met, dated, and courted her now husband, he generated a six-figure income. Once they were married, he was still able to provide for the family and take care of the home, even though he brought in less income than his wife. She purchased their home using her earnings, but he was responsible for all the bills within the home. Although she paid the mortgage, he paid the electricity, gas, lawn care, insurance, water, sewage, maintenance, HOA fees, groceries, house cleaning costs, etc. She was not taking care of him while he contributed only the bare minimum. They found a way to split the financial responsibilities within their home so that he could still provide for and take care of his family.

In conclusion, I am going to give you a scripture reference list to help you build your faith in your standards and desires. The most important and powerful thing you can do when you are not sure if you are indeed being too picky or not is to seek God in prayer. Hear from him and go from there. Also, remember who exactly God is. He is an Ephesians 3:20 God. He over-delivers. If he wants you to tweak or adjust your standards or desires, he would want you to ask for his very best, not water down your belief and your faith. Maybe you're not asking for enough. Perhaps your faith is falling short of God's will for your life. When the Lord is involved with your love life, it is always going to be better than you are expecting.

Your mind, body, and soul matter when it comes to your spiritual and natural standards. You will have greater peace in the dating season when you choose to trust God over what you may not see with your eyes. You will have increased joy when the Lord connects you with exactly the type of man you prayed for. You will have greater peace when you are dating only the high-caliber type of men you actually want to date because you have not settled just to get a date. You also will be able to keep the personal promises you have made to God regarding your celibacy and spiritual growth, including time in prayer, study, worship, and service when you refuse to get close to a man who is not on the same spiritual page as you are.

What you want matters. What you need matters. The path that the Lord has you on is important. Continue to trust God to send you an amazing man who will love you as Christ loves the church, covers your family spiritually and financially, and is attractive, even handsome in your eyes. Read and study these scripture references to build your faith:

Psalm 37:4, Proverbs 10:24, Mark 11:24, Psalm 145:19, Lamentations 3:25, Philippians 4:19, John 15:7 & 16, Habakkuk 2:2-4, Hebrews 11:1, 1 John 5:14-15, Matthew 21:22, John 16:23-24.

RULE #3:

IF IT DOESN'T FIT, DON'T FORCE IT

When you try on a shoe that's one size too small, what happens? It hurts. Your foot is uncomfortable and in pain. You can't walk straight or properly. If you're able to run, it will only be a very short distance, before the pain of trying to force a smaller shoe to fit on a larger foot becomes too much. What if the shoe is too big? You may not be in pain, yet you still will not be able to maneuver properly or effectively. You will be tripping; the shoe will probably fall off and get left behind. Not to mention, the shoe will not be visually appealing since it will be disproportionate compared to the rest of your body.

This is how it looks and feels when you try to force a relationship or man to fit into your life (or you to fit into his) when there are clear signs that you two are not a complement to each other. There may be pain and awkwardness and the natural blessed flow of a God-ordained relationship is missing.

When the Lord connects you with the husband he desires you to marry, your lives will fit and flow together very well. If the relationship feels forced, no matter what stage you are in, that is a sign. If you have to convince a male friend that you should be more than friends, it doesn't fit. If you have to "make" a boyfriend see that you are a wife, it doesn't fit. If you have to force relationship progression, it doesn't fit. God is not the author of confusion, but of peace (1 Corinthians 14:33).

HIGHLIGHT THIS: When you are dating and building a relationship with a man, if you are on a path towards marriage (or considering that path), your lives should fit together like a puzzle. Think of every aspect of your lives as separate puzzle pieces and how the entire picture of married life would look if all of those pieces culminated together. When the two become one, two single persons' lives join together in an eternal spiritual and natural bond. It's true that your decision making will change as you consider the other person and adjustments will be made on both sides to accommodate the other.

Yet, right now in your singleness, each of your lives is already flowing in a certain manner, heading in a specific direction. You each have a plan or vision for your future with goals and desires. Even as you consider factoring each other into your future endeavors, you should not have to turn your world upside down or give up all hopes, dreams, and wishes just to enter into a marriage. God has called you to a life of peace (Malachi 2:5).

LET'S PIECE THE PICTURE TOGETHER

Here are different pieces of your lives that should fit together like a puzzle to create the complete vision of your future together.

Spiritual Piece (1 Corinthians 5:9-13) Are both people on the same level and path, spiritually speaking? We have already established that the man must be saved. Now think about his spiritual maturity, worship, giving, understanding, and life application of the Word of God. If you hear from God, does he also hear God's voice? If you are filled with the Holy Spirit and pray in tongues, has he also received this gift? If the Word of God is your foundation and final authority, does it hold the same weight and reverence in his life? When there is a misunderstanding or discussion about the interpretation of doctrine or scripture, how will it be resolved? How you both view, submit to, honor, and serve religious authority is a major piece of your individual lives that must fit together comfortably as you build the full puzzle picture of your future life together.

Lifestyle Piece (1 Timothy 2:1-2) Do you both live peaceful and godly lifestyles? When it comes to work, leisure, and family time, consider whether and how you will enjoy life together. Even though you may have different preferences for entertainment and recreation, will you still be glorifying God in your fun? Discuss what will be most important when it comes to not only raising the children (we will discuss this more later) but also what family worship and fun time will be like. What about your work beliefs and habits? Are you on the same page when it comes to work-life balance?

Money Piece (Matthew 22:21) Not only is the man's ability to provide for his family important but also how you both earn, manage, invest, spend, give and distribute financial resources is of utmost importance. Will you be able to maintain a similar or better quality of life when the two households are combined into one? Do you both share the same beliefs concerning giving and tithing into the kingdom of God? You may want to decide who will be the primary money manager in the home during the courtship process, but for now, think about how he invests and spends his money as a single man and what that would look like once your entire family is affected by his financial decisions.

Life Purpose & Calling Piece (Jeremiah 1:5) Since God's ultimate purpose for marriage is to glorify him, you both will be able to serve God at your best together. As a helpmate, you should be able to help your man go higher in his purpose. This is not the same as dictating, managing, and governing his purpose, which is the job of the Holy Spirit inside of him. When you think about the purpose and calling of both of your individual lives, would they flow well together when you join your lives? Are your purpose, calling, and spiritual gifts able to sync with grace, peace, and anointing? Your purpose and calling do not need to match, but they must complement each other.

Even though you may have amazing chemistry with a man, that does not mean your lives are meant to combine into one. When the two become one, you will have one vision, one goal, one focus for the entire family. Don't try to force a fit. Keep these words in mind: complement, flow, peace, and harmony. Trust that the Lord will send you a spouse with whom the pieces all fit together perfectly like a puzzle.

 AMOS 3:3 (New King James Version) Can two walk together, unless they are agreed?

RULE #4:

TRUST YOUR DISCERNMENT

I believe the Lord has blessed women with strong discernment in dating for our own protection (Hebrews 5:14). The world likes to call this discernment "a woman's intuition" or "trusting your gut." I prefer to give our Creator all the glory and praise him for the inward leadership as the Holy Spirit communicates with our own spirits and provides supernatural direction in relationships. Give yourself permission to trust your discernment. Our words and behaviors are clues into our true beliefs, feelings, and state of mind. Body language and non-verbal communication are important.

I am not saying that we should be paranoid or distrusting, women of God. Most of the time we have no problem discerning the good in men we are dating and seeing the potential they have. We desire to think the best of them and give the benefit of the doubt to the amazing man we learn about as we build a friendship. During the initial friendship phase of the dating relationship, each person is putting their best foot forward to impress the other and it takes some time to peel back the layers.

Think about the last time you were dating someone and noticed subtle or blatant behaviors that triggered your discernment. Did you listen to your discernment or talk yourself out of what your spirit was sensing? What was the end result of that situation?

I remember when I made the decision to begin trusting my discernment and never allow anyone to talk me out of my inner witness. When a boyfriend was not being truthful regarding other women, whether it was inappropriate,  line-crossing behavior, or outright cheating, my spirit would always discern what was "unsaid." Words that were unspoken, mixed messages, or incomplete explanations gave my heart and mind cues that something was wrong. They were not clues (as I was not looking to figure anything out), but cues — strong hints that I should not give my heart to the man in question because he was not trustworthy. Each time these men would claim that I had trust issues and they weren't hiding anything. Yet, a little while later (weeks and sometimes days later) the full truth would unfold and confirm that in fact, my discernment was correct.

SCAN ME

Watch the Discernment in Dating video and learn how to grow your spiritual sensitivity.

You may also be a prophetic woman of God, in which case your discernment is heightened and the Lord may give you dreams and visions revealing the inward character of a man or even actions or behaviors he is hiding (Hebrews 4:12). One example I have concerns the time when the Lord gave me a vision on the very first date I had with a man that revealed the current state of his heart. He was a broken man, not whole emotionally or spiritually, yet giving the outward appearance of being ready for a serious relationship. Although he denied what was going on with him when I asked probing questions, after the relationship began to fail, he admitted that he was not ready for a real relationship with me or anyone else.

Another example is when I was having a disagreement with a man I was in a relationship with over the phone, I was able to see the demonic spirit that was influencing his mind and thinking. The spirit was literally attached to his mind. I prayed for him right away, yet I understand that when demonic spirits are involved, the person needs to renounce and break ties with those spirits on their own in order to be fully delivered. As long as that person is in agreement with the spirit (even unknowingly) that spirit has the power to keep the individual bound. In this case, my man-friend did not see anything wrong or any need for deliverance; he believed his thinking and responses based on his thought life were valid. However, God was showing me what was in store for our relationship if I decided to go all-in with a man who maintained an unchanging belief system and mindset.

TRUST ISSUES VS. DISCERNMENT

2 PETER 1:21 (NKJV) for prophecy never came by the will of man, but [a]holy men of God spoke as they were moved by the Holy Spirit.

While I am a huge proponent of following your discernment, I also understand that there is a distinct difference between having discernment and having trust issues. While both unctions are birthed from within your spirit, the driving force and primary initiator behind each option determines their viability. When you begin questioning a man's motives or actions, not based on the individual or specific circumstances, but rather based on your personal history with men or a failed prior relationship, you may have trust issues. Accusations that stem from what you have witnessed take place in other relationships around you, in your family, or even in your own bloodline are unfair and are a sign that inner spiritual, emotional, and mental healing and forgiveness may be necessary before you seriously begin dating for marriage.

The scripture reference found in 2 Peter 1:21 is speaking specifically about a word of prophecy which is different from spiritual discernment, yet the principle remains. When a message is imparted into our spirit from heaven, it is given only by the Holy Spirit himself, not by the will of man or because you are trying to find a reason not to believe or trust the man you are dating.

Consider how you talk about men when you are not currently dating. What do you believe about men and their behavior towards women? What types of fears do you have about entering into a new relationship? Do you enter relationships subconsciously waiting for the "other shoe to drop"? If you begin to side-eye a man when he literally has not had any red-flag-giving behavior, you are not receiving any direction from deep within your spirit (only from inside your head), and the relationship started off well and is maintaining a healthy flow, work on resting and trusting God.

Honesty and self-reflection are necessary to ensure that you don't sabotage your own relationship or push a good man away. My number one recommendation is to get counseling not only from your girlfriend or mom (although I know how intensely insightful they can be) but to talk to a professional, licensed counselor or therapist, preferably a Christian one. I do not recommend simply submitting a prayer request to your church or even meeting with a minister. Those are one-time events that may feel good in the moment but will not help you with the inner spiritual and emotional work you need to do to remove those trust issues with men permanently and begin to fully trust in God. You need to understand not only the place where those issues stem from but how to work through the process of personal growth before you enter into a new relationship, so that it will be as peaceful and blessed as possible.

RULE #5:

ENSURE YOUR PARENTING STYLES ARE A MATCH

I f we lived in a perfectly biblical society, men and women would be raised in homes with a Christian foundation, living out the uncompromised and living Word of God. It would be normal for all boys, girls and young adults to be virgins, since there would be no fornication or normalization of young/premarital sex as societies have become accustomed to at large today.

For this reason, when a man would court and marry a woman, they both would be virgins and experience parenthood for the first time together. The parents they would become to their children would be based on principles of Christ-centered family focus (such as godly vision for the home, discipleship and fulfilling the Great Commission) as well as loving each other not based on mere emotion but based on God's definition of love clearly stated in 1 Corinthians 13:4-8. A Christian home would be a place of worship, agape love, and kingdom focus and service.

Divorce would be uncommon and rare as couples would be led by God in the dating and courting process, while each single man and woman continued to live their lives for the glory of God. The success of marriage would be due, not to the perfection of humans, but to the foundation of Christ in not only the individual's upbringing, but also the relationship and the marriage itself.

The abundance of single parents as a direct result of premarital unprotected sex was never God's intention.

SIDE BAR: I am NOT saying that these children are not in God's plan. I am NOT saying that any of these children are a mistake. I am NOT saying that Christ-centered homes are perfect. I am NOT saying divorce cannot occur in a Christ-centered home. I am NOT saying that all children belonging to single parents are a result of premarital sex. Also, I do not have a judgmental stance on this topic, as I, myself am an unmarried mother, as a result of premarital sex at the time of the writing of this book. I believe in the redemptive character trait and power of Christ and the fact that no one is perfect. When we repent, Christ is waiting with open arms to welcome us back into the fold of godliness and purpose.

With that being said, the way each person approaches single parenting should be based on a Christian perspective. After teaching, serving, and ministering to Christian women for over a decade, I have learned that the term Christian can be used rather loosely, and is relative to the individual's experiences, background and understanding. When believers of Christ were first identified as Christians it was based on the outsiders' observance of their behavior. Before they became known as Christians (Acts 11:26), they were simply called Christ followers and/or disciples. What separated Christ's followers from other faiths in the region is written clearly throughout the book of Acts. The disciples not only followed Christ before he was crucified, but they followed Christ's pattern of living. Christians were known for preaching about Christ, performing miracles, signs and wonders by the power of the Holy Spirit, and converting non-believers into faith-filled followers of Christ Jesus through salvation.

Therefore it is clear, based on scripture, that a Christian is someone who:

♥   Preaches and teaches the message of Christ (who he is and what he has done)

♥   Performs miracles, signs and wonders in the name of Jesus Christ (John 14:12, Mark 16:17)

♥   Ministers salvation unto conversion

These are the exact works of the disciples, at the point that they became identified as Christians, to set them apart from other disciples of false gods and faiths.

What does all this have to do with single parenting? This book is written to provide biblical principles of love, dating and relationships with the goal of readers entering into a God-glorifying marriage. As such, when it comes to parenting styles, not only should you examine the man of God you are dating's parenting style and ability, but also your own.

Let's say either of you have children already. Be honest with yourself about how he parents his children and how he will act as a leader of a household if you get married. Don't think only about his ability to be an amazing husband, but truly consider the type of father he will be. If either of you have children now, you have the opportunity to preview his beliefs and parenting style before you get too deep into the relationship. Through gentle conversations in addition to observation, you can identify what he believes about discipline, education, play, relationships and how to instill godly principles through parenting. You will also learn what he believes about parenting children in a blended family.

Remember, that if his children are older or adults, he might not desire to parent your future children together in the same manner. Since you were also not the other parent involved with the raising of those children, the outcome will be different when you two are married and raising children together.

When it comes to what parenting choices will be deal breakers and which will be negotiable, that is entirely up to you. What should be true for all Christians is that creating an atmosphere of agape love with worship and service to God is a bare minimum. The lifestyle that each adult adopts pertaining to godliness will be naturally observed and incorporated into the lives of young children, even without much effort from the parents. For example, if the children witness parents praising and worshipping God regularly, they too will begin to praise and worship God using similar cues they have witnessed. Just like patterns are used in schools to help children learn, young minds will learn based on Christian patterns followed in the home. Some lessons such as financial literacy, managing conflict with the love of God, peace and wisdom, and how to serve, minister and share the message of Christ must be taught intentionally and instilled in children.

MY PERSONAL EXPERIENCE

When I was 35 years of age and in a relationship with a 44-year-old gentleman, our mindset differences pertaining to raising children came up on more than one occasion. The first concern arose when discussing his teenage children from his failed marriage. I asked him about financially supporting his children post-graduation in their college or training endeavors. He replied that he didn't believe in giving his children any money once they were grown (18 years of age) because they needed to learn to make it on their own. He stated they needed to learn "the struggle" and also that no one had helped him early in life. He believed that helping his children with college expenses was giving them a handout. I then began to inquire about what he believed about adding his children to his retirement plan so that he could pass down a financial inheritance, to which his reply was pretty much the same. He didn't believe in giving any money to his children after they were grown, even though he admitted previously that he was currently receiving so much increased income, he was not sure exactly what he would do with the extra money. This is actually how the conversation started in the first place.

My parenting mindset is that if there is increased financial wherewithal to the point that you "have so much money you don't know what to do with it," it should be set aside for the kiddos. Whether they use it for college, a business endeavor, or to make real estate investments or purchase their first property, if you can afford to give your children a financial foundation you yourself did not have, go ahead and provide it for them. I could go into great detail about the lack of financial literacy and wealth management in the African American community, but I will stick to the spiritual focus of this book. It is stated in scripture that a good man leaves an inheritance to his children's children (Proverbs 13:22). When one does a full study of the Word of God, it is found that men would teach their children to carry on the family's business and God-given assignment. The grandchildren would inherit literally everything, including money. This is true whether expressly acknowledged or not. We each have inherited a generational curse or a generational blessing or both through our family bloodlines.

Towards the end of this relationship, there was a second incident that took place as we were traveling together on a short mini-vacation to the oceanfront. At the time my son had just turned three, and we were chilling in the hotel suite at dusk. As it neared his bedtime, I turned off one of the lights that was near my son's bed in the room and my man-friend started to complain that he couldn't see. All of the lights in the room were not off, so it wasn't pitch black, just on the side where my son's bed was. I asked him whether he expected me to leave the lights on and not to put my child to sleep. He said that my son wasn't going to sleep anyway. I knew in that moment that he expected me to serve his needs over my son's and if it meant my toddler was going to be up late, cranky and overtired (young mothers know that this is not good for either the kids or the parents), but he didn't care; his only concern was what he wanted to do. I literally had to make a choice between comforting my child so he could go to sleep or entertaining my man. I chose to take care of my child and felt very strongly that this small matter was a sign of what was in store. I was correct.

The next day we went out to the oceanfront. After playing in the water and building sandcastles, my son fell asleep, cozied up on the beach blanket under the umbrella. We sat and chatted for about 15 minutes and then my man-friend said, "I'm hungry. I'm ready to go." I told him that my son just fell asleep and I didn't want to wake him up, nor could I carry him back to the hotel suite (we were on the 20th floor and about ½ mile down the oceanfront). We had a bunch of stuff with us, and my toddler was a big boy.

Two minutes later, my man-friend started packing up everything (including the umbrella) and was heading off the beach. Yet I hadn't moved an inch. I looked at him in shock. I couldn't believe he was going to leave us in the hot sun. I did not think asking him to wait 30 more minutes was asking too much. We exchanged a few more words and since he had left his car keys in the hotel suite, I had no choice. I grabbed our things, picked up my baby and started trekking to the 20th floor. Needless to say, I was extremely frustrated and upset. I didn't come out of my character; I remained calm and kind, but I marked that moment in my mind.

It was evident after those two moments that his man would always expect me to place his needs over my child's needs and that even though he wanted to be with me, he did not view me as a package deal. You can tell when a man is very into you individually and simply tolerates your children but does not really love or care for them. I grew up in a home that functioned in that manner and I had no intention of creating that type of environment for my child. Don't get me wrong, I do believe that he wouldn't intentionally harm my son, however, he wouldn't proactively love him either, which is just as damaging. Children need to feel loved in a home.

I was not expecting him to love my son after being together for only 6 months, and meeting my child a few months in. However, I was expecting him to understand my need as a new mother to make sure my toddler was taken care of without giving me an attitude or putting me in a position to be forced to choose between providing the best childcare and pleasing him.

Again, these types of issues that arise during a relationship are just a preview of what lies ahead if you continue on a deeper journey with the person. Just like your lives should fit together, so should both of your parenting styles.

Let's say neither of you have children. In my opinion this is the best scenario. You both lack experience with child rearing, so you can learn together. Neither of you will assume you know more than the other or have presumptions based on past relationships and parenting experiences. Don't get me wrong; experience with children can be beneficial but sometimes, it can be a roadblock to progress if one person is not open to thinking and maneuvering differently in a manner that works for the new relationship you are building together.

Here are some things to consider when learning about the compatibility of your two parenting styles:

- Discipline, punishment, and positive reinforcement

- Conflict resolution

- Education, schooling, life planning

- Roles and responsibilities, work-life balance, and rotations

- Financial planning, management, and investing

- Spiritual teaching, guidance and leadership at home (in addition to attending church services)

- Navigating a co-parenting arrangement, if needed

I have one last real-life example to share with you that should drive home the point of this biblical rule to godly dating. I was in a relationship with a man who I believed had an inappropriate relationship with his children's mom (at the time I had no children of my own). Because I did not have any children, I was slow to speak about my feelings and I was very, very patient and understanding. While it is good to be patient and understanding, it is not wise to bite your tongue and bury your true feelings, because your thoughts and instincts may be valid.

In this case, we were in a long-distance relationship, but he came to town quite frequently, at least once or twice a month. When he would come to town prior to the start of our official relationship, he would stay at his children's mother's home for a week or two at a time. Although he claimed there was nothing intimate taking place, once we entered into a relationship officially, I thought it would be understood that this behavior was not acceptable or respectful to any woman that is his girlfriend. Most women would run for the hills, as I should have done during the friendship phase, instead of continuing to consider and pursue a relationship in light of such a situation.

Now, because he saw nothing wrong with not only spending weeks at a time at her house when he came into town, but also dropping everything while we were on dates to run to her house if the children were misbehaving, once we were officially in a committed relationship, he thought that I would be okay with this behavior and my disapproval led to many intense arguments. No matter how much I explained that although I didn't have children or a baby daddy, I personally knew of co-parenting relationships that were organized and peaceful and did not require the man to spend the night at the home, even for one night. These co-parents did not require or expect the other parent to drop everything when they called to rush to the other person's house because the children were not perfectly obedient in a moment. He would also have lengthy personal conversations on the phone with her about topics that had nothing to do with the children at all. He informed me that no matter what she needed or when she needed it, she could always call him, whether it was about the children or not. This sounds crazy, even as I share this story with you today.

When I addressed my concerns with his own mother, assuming she would talk to her son about appropriate behavior since he is officially in a committed relationship, she led me to believe that this was a culturally acceptable behavior, because he had witnessed his own father come to spend weeks at a time with her to help out with the children, even while he was married to another woman. However, in American culture, we call that having a second family. So this relationship had to end because we could never see eye to eye on what was and what was not acceptable co-parenting behavior. Our beliefs and mindsets did not complement each other at all, which was a clear sign this was not the God-ordained relationship the Lord had in store for me.

RULE #6:

SPIRITUAL MATURITY IS A TWO-WAY STREET

There is a time when you are in the best state mentally, emotionally and spiritually to date. In fact, when you have worked on yourself as a woman and grown to an amazing place in your relationship with God, these are sign posts to locate that indicate you are truly ready to date. You are not perfect by any means, but your life is peaceful, blessed and fruitful in many ways.

As I begin teaching about the way to proceed while examining the fruit of the life of the man of God you are dating, I want to be sure that you first undergo some honest self-reflection on where you are in your own life as far as fruitfulness is concerned.

The Bible tells us that we can judge a tree by its fruit (Matthew 7:16-27). Jesus also stated how important it is that we first examine our own lives, not from a place of condemnation, but to ensure we don't get so wrapped up pointing out to others "flaws that we fail to acknowledge" and work on our own (Matthew 7:3-5). For this reason, to show fairness and balance, I will walk you through various aspects of examining fruitfulness throughout the man of God's life, while also helping you to consider and realize your own fruitfulness.

The most important area to begin with is spiritual maturity. Modern Christendom has made spiritual maturity very subjective, when in fact we can utilize clearly stated scriptures to identify true spiritual maturity in an objective manner. Additionally, true righteous judgment (John 7:24) is based on the Word of God, not on worldly perspectives or philosophies.

THE FRUIT OF THE SPIRIT OR THE WORKS OF THE FLESH

The last 10 verses in Galatians Chapter 5 provide a wonderful contrast of what it means to walk in the Spirit versus living in the flesh. The key in maintaining balance in understanding whether a person is spiritually immature or growing through progressive sanctification, is the individual's continual desire followed by corresponding actions to grow in the fruit of the Spirit. In other words, when a person is set in their carnal ways, they will operate in their flesh with no remorse or conviction to change. Now when a person not only acknowledges their weaknesses in the flesh, but puts forth real, regular effort towards growth, the Lord will assist and accelerate their spiritual growth.

There is a difference between a transgression (making one-off mistakes) and living in iniquity (habitual sin). Don't be fooled by a man who claims he is trying to do better yet has no actions to support his statements. Also be careful not to read into a man of God's behavior and assume he is being convicted towards repentance, when in fact he is comfortable in a sinful, carnal lifestyle of the flesh.

Adding balance, you also want to ensure that you are following the leadership of the Holy Spirit and growing stronger in the fruit of the Spirit and weaker in the works of the flesh. It is counterproductive to get into a close relationship with someone who shares the same sinful behavior and carnal mindset as you do. The man will distract you and keep you stuck in place. As you both feed into each other's weaknesses and condone behavior unproductive to the spirit, not only will you be unable to make strides with God, but your relationship will not suddenly become a God-glorifying one that leads to a blessed marriage that yields a reflection of the Body of Christ (Ephesians Chapter 5).

Galatians 5:19-21 tells us that the works of the flesh are evident. In other words, they are crystal clear, plainly stated, and require no interpretation.

WORKS OF THE FLESH: IMMORAL WAYS, FILTHY THOUGHTS, AND SHAMEFUL DEEDS

- Idol worship
- Witchcraft
- Hate of others and being difficult to get along with
- Jealousy and envy
- Quick temper and anger
- Argumentative attitude
- Trouble Makers
- Drunkards
- Wild Partiers
- Other works of evil (behaviors and traits that are not within the nature of God)

On the flip side, when the Holy Spirit is alive and moving on the inside of someone's spirit, there is change, growth and transformation towards godliness. Fruit is the external evidence of the work of the Holy Spirit on the inside of a person's born-again spirit.

FRUIT OF THE SPIRIT: LIFE AND UNSELFISH FEELINGS, DESIRES AND BEHAVIORS

- Loving (as defined by 1 Corinthians 13:4-8)
- Joyful and happy
- Peaceful
- Patient
- Kind
- Good and gentle
- Faithful
- Self-controlled

GODLINESS = BEING LIKE CHRIST

A simple way to determine godliness is to examine and understand the life of Christ by conducting a thorough study of the synoptic gospels. The attributes, characteristics, traits, and lifestyle of Christ should be our guide always to keep us on track.

If you were to align your life and daily decisions with the life of Christ and do a side-by-side comparison, how much overlap would you see? Do you have many similarities? In unique situations, do you employ the same thought process that Christ himself had? Do you have a "kingdom first" perspective? Are you focused on and submitted to the will of God even above your own personal will and desires?

Jesus was and is always focused on reaching souls, serving people and teaching the precepts of God. It is true that we don't have much documentation of his family or personal life, but God provided enough insight through documented stories for us to model the life of Christ, even as it relates to our own family and personal life.

Before we dive into handling a relationship as Christ would, let's first take a look at how you and the man of interest are both living your lives in a Christ-like manner as two singles. Godliness is revealed not only in words, but in action. Private and public behavior are the reflection of the true character and heart of a person.

I have made the mistake in the past of assuming a person had a strong, private and quiet relationship with God, with serious prayer, worship and study...but they just didn't talk about it often. When the same person would display public actions that opposed Christ's position in lifestyle, decision-making, and relationship management, I would make excuses for them and chalk it up to imperfect human behavior.

At some point during our interactions (whether this person was a family member, romantic interest, or coaching client), I would have the undeniable realization that this person simply was not godly or Christ-like at all, although they were indeed Christian. There was no private and quiet relationship with the Holy Spirit never expressed or spoken of. Sadly, the intimate relationship (inclusive of prayer, study, and regular worship) was missing altogether. Here's the proof: when you have a close relationship with someone, you talk about them. You bring them up and mention them in regular conversation. Although a spiritually mature person may not share the entirety of personal revelations and encounters they have with the Holy Spirit, they will certainly mention the fact that they are having these experiences, as they are a regular part of their life.

When I am coaching a client and she spends 20-30 minutes straight talking about a specific man or relationship issue, but does not mention the Lord, not even once in the conversation, I already know that her relationship with God is minimal or non-existent. Most of the concerns and issues she has would be mitigated through an enhancement of her spiritual life, which would then lead to godliness and spiritual growth. For example, better discernment, obedience, and submission to God's Word would discourage you from giving your heart to the wrong man and ending up with a broken heart and spirit. Understanding more about who Christ is and modeling his behavior would also reduce confusion and poor decision making based on physical and natural desires without considering the spiritual ramifications.

When it comes to modeling Christ in love and dating relationships, godly dating is evident when the kingdom of God is a priority in the individual's life and when romantic relationship choices are based on the will and desires of God. How Christ would handle himself in a relationship is exactly how we should govern ourselves. Christ would remain holy and not fornicate. Christ would prioritize his service to God, while also making time for love. Granted, Christ was called to a life of singleness, but if he had the option to get married, he would still prioritize the kingdom of God, even as he made room for marital love. Likewise, you (and the man you are dating) should still spend time with the Holy Spirit in prayer and worship, study the scriptures for daily understanding and application and serve people to bring them into the kingdom of God in your own way. A spiritually mature person does not throw their entire walk with God in the toilet once they are seriously dating. Christ himself would not operate that way. This is the true definition of godly dating.

FILLED WITH AND LED BY GOD'S SPIRIT

I have taught for years about creating a written list of the characteristics, qualities, and attributes you desire in a future husband to use as a faith tool. This is not to place yourself in a box, but rather to help guide your dating choices by writing out your non-negotiables and your greatest desires in a description of your future husband.

One day, while discussing the fact that my list had 27 items on it, my mother said, "Well Sarita, if he is like Christ, a lot of those things would already be included." She was right.

As I began praying for a Christ-like man of God and remained on the dating scene with so-called Christian men, my prayer changed again. The Lord took me to Romans 8:14 and showed me how to tell whether a man was truly Christ-like and had a true relationship with the Holy Spirit or not. It had everything to do with whether the man was led by the Holy Spirit, day by day, moment by moment, or if he had a form of godliness but denied the power of God unto sanctification.

Additionally, when it came to how a man would treat me as a woman, there are obvious behaviors that a man truly led by the Spirit of God would or would not do. Not that our dealings would be perfect, but the Lord would be involved in not only leading me in how to communicate with, respect and honor him as a man, but leading him in how to cherish, love and respect me as a woman. Again, mistakes and misunderstandings will happen here and there but when your spirit is led by God's Spirit, there will be peace, love and truth in the relationship. The nature of Christ will be evident between you.

Let's state this even more plainly. A man led by God's Spirit would not convince you to break your celibacy walk because they would already have the revelation of fleeing fornication (1 Corinthians 6:18). A man led by God's Spirit wouldn't cheat because he would be convicted by the Holy Spirit at the onset of an inappropriate relationship with another woman and would take actions to distance himself from crossing any lines. A man led by God's Spirit would not lose his temper and abuse a woman in any manner (Colossians 3:19). A man led by God's Spirit would not twist or manipulate scriptures to meet his own wants and needs and/or manipulate women.

A man and woman who are both led by God's Spirit will operate with the wisdom of God, fruit of the Spirit and the agape love of God (based on 1 Corinthians 13:4-8). Neither party is perfect, yet they both do their best to honor God in their dealings with each other. Simply being a Christian is not enough when it comes to spiritual maturity. Being led by God's Spirit is what separates those who have a lip service form of godliness but are not truly living their lives in communion and unison with the Holy Spirit.

RULE #7:

EXAMINE THE FRUIT OF HIS LIFE

I started off the previous chapter showing you how vital it is to examine the fruit in a man of God's life as well as having honest moments of transparency regarding your own fruitfulness. We have covered spiritual fruit examination in detail and now we will delve into the natural fruit.

Think of natural fruit as harvest. It is the external and tangible evidence that someone's life is producing because of certain seeds they have sown over time. It is therefore the harvest that is produced in various seasons of an individual's life. No matter what is going on in someone's life, they have sown seeds and are now living in the midst of their harvest. As adults, we take responsibility and are accountable for the choices we have made in every area of our life that have led us to a certain destination. Even when unpredictable circumstances arise, the way we respond with our action or inaction will determine where we eventually end up.

Since you are a woman of God who is dating for the purpose of marriage, it's important that you maintain a balanced perspective to determine if he will be a good husband and father while leaving room for grace. Remember also that while there are areas that you will work on together as a couple during premarital counseling, certain foundational aspects of a man's life should be firmly established prior to even considering whether he is someone you would want to take the leap with. Likewise, certain foundational aspects of your own life should be firmly established prior to considering becoming someone's wife and mother.

HIGHLIGHT THIS: It is not wise to build a future based on "potential" alone. The potential you see is not a solid foundation to build a marriage upon. Often women (including myself) have made many excuses for the bad fruit in a man's life for the sake of "potential." We want the best, think the best and desire to be married...soon. Therefore, we will disregard blatant red flags or think that our prayers will fix, motivate, or inspire a man to live up to the potential we see with our own imagination. Never mind what he, himself has expressed as short-term and long-term goals. How many snares of the enemy have you found yourself in with past relationships that were built on potential, instead of mutually agreed upon measurable goals? Don't repeat the same mistakes.

The following are some key areas to consider during fruit examination.

LIVING ARRANGEMENT

There are all kinds of living arrangements a person may have. Remember however, that you are dating for marriage and determining if a man of God is truly husband material or not.

I remember a time in my late twenties when I was interested in a guy at my church. I shared with my good friend sentiments about my crush, and she quickly declared, "Sarita, he has a roommate." I tilted my head and drew breath to respond with a hesitant, "Well..." and she interrupted, "You need a real man." My friend was right. I was at a point in my life where I had a good job, a car that was paid for, and a cute, spacious 2-bedroom apartment. That was the same year I sold my first home and moved to a new state. A grown man with a roommate was obviously at a different place in his life.

Let's fast forward to my thirties. One man I was in a relationship with lived with his family, which he claimed was due to their culture. Family members, even adults, no matter how old, would live together and not move out on their own. Another man lived with his mother, as he claimed he needed to move back in to help her raise his 10 orphaned nieces and nephews. Another man lived with his aunt for unknown reasons, and yet another lived with his father because he had broken up with his fiancée, whom he shared a home with, but when they broke up, he decided to put all his things in storage and move in with his dad. This is quite the roster I know.

These men's ages ranged from mid-thirties to mid-forties. This is an important detail because none of these men were college students or even graduate students. Now if this book was written for late teens, early twenty-something women who were dating young men, these living arrangements would be more acceptable and understandable. If both the young man and the young woman were in college or just starting out in life, coming into adulthood, they could both live with other people, date, court, marry, move into their first home on their own together and begin building a life and raising a young family. My guess is, you are not about 21 years old, the men you are dating are not 21, 22 or 23 years of age either. You are a mature woman, desiring a mature man.

While experiencing a real honest moment with myself after ending the relationship with the man who lived with his dad, I had to acknowledge a few truths. Number one: if a man has an odd and "special" living arrangement, there are major underlying issues about why his life was producing the fruit of instability. Sometimes you can piece together the heart of the matter if you are patient enough to uncover the real reason behind the seeds sown in his life that result in such a harvest. Number two: I had to understand why I kept being so understanding that I continued to move forward and engage in relationships with these types of men when having his own home should be a non-negotiable factor for a woman who has obtained any level of her own success. I had sown enough seeds in my life to learn how to move out of my mom's house at 18 and purchase two homes by the age of 34. I never had a roommate, lived with family or hit such a rough patch that I couldn't take care of myself. I even had a season in which I made the poor choice of renting a home that was out of my income bracket, was forced to break the lease I couldn't afford, and still managed to downgrade into a more reasonably priced home, on my own. Number three: I had to get honest about 1) why I thought I was being too picky for expecting a man to have himself together, and 2) where my faith was weak about the type of man God would connect me with who would become my future husband.

Let's think about this subjectively. If a man has a living arrangement that is questionable, there is a reason. You may or may not ever uncover the real reason behind the seeds he has sown to land him in his current living situation, but you are merely responsible for your mindset, belief, faith and how you choose to move forward with him. I understand that everyone has a different background and life experiences. Again, the choices we make as we maneuver through life are leaving seeds planted along the way which will produce a harvest. The seeds left by this sort of man usually look like a lack of consistency, integrity, and stability.

If a man's life is in flux, he is currently unstable and not ready to marry and create a foundation for a new family with you. If a man lacks integrity, discipline, and self-control, he may be unable to maintain regular, solid employment to pay rent. How would this person be able to pay a mortgage when you two get married and want to build a life? If a man simply does not generate enough income to be able to support one person (himself), how will he be able to support a growing family, even though you two will decide how bills will be shared? These are also the types of men who tend to treat women poorly. Of course, this is not a blanket statement about all men in these situations, but nine times out of ten, this will be the case.

If a man has planted seeds of working consistently, learning to pay his own bills regularly and house, feed and clothe himself once he entered full adulthood, he would then have the harvest of a stable and blessed living arrangement. A husband looking to find his wife has his life in order for his next season.

FINANCIAL STABILITY

Similar to being clear and honest about a man's living arrangement is the transparency and realization concerning his financial stability. Only in recent years has this become the subject of a much-needed conversation, as women have been either deceived by or simply okay with the lack of financial stability possessed by a man. Before we delve into how to examine a man's financial fruitfulness, I want to explain the importance of being on the same page concerning the generation and management of monetary resources.

Let me preface it by saying that this topic has nothing to do with being a gold-digger or dating only men who are rich. If you're reading this book, odds are you are not living in poverty and you're also not a billionaire. You are a professional woman somewhere in between who desires to marry a man who is either your equal financially or on a higher playing field financially. This desire is not wrong.

Let's check the history books. One thousand years ago it was understood that a man provides for his family. Let's check the Word of God. Even though the Proverbs 31 woman was a strong-willed entrepreneur, her husband was still the head of the home. Again, we don't have any biblical story where the husband was at home with the kids and the woman went out to work to provide for the family.

I am also not saying that a woman can't make more money than a man. However, if the financial or income discrepancy is too wide, the relationship will have difficulties. The differences in how two people generate, manage, spend, invest, and give (into the house of God, into people's lives personally and to charitable endeavors) plays a large role in the peaceful flow of the relationship.

Here's how it looks when there are extreme financial differences. One person is ready to invest in real estate and the other has no savings account and therefore no experience with disciplined saving towards a major investment. One person has worked with their company for 15 years, the other is in between jobs every 2 to 3 years. One person has a growing whole life insurance policy, mutual fund account and/or 401K account and therefore is prepared for hard times with multiple ways to stay afloat financially in a crisis. The other person does not even have an emergency fund. One person is investing in the stock market and getting pretty good results while the other person spends all earned income down to the last dollar and can't even discuss investing in any way, shape or form.

Now, let's talk about quality of life due to financial disparity. If one person has previously or currently owns multiple properties, but the other person (the man in this case) is still living with another person because they can't afford rent on their own, these two individuals have a different quality of life in multiple ways. If one person takes first class vacations and purchases high-end products and the other person is on a very limited budget (constrained by their own personal income), they may view the other person's normal way of living as wasteful or frivolous. When it comes time to plan for retirement, transition in your career, or enroll the children in private school and college, there will be many disagreements and much head bumping. Even when it comes to organic, all-natural food versus discount grocery food, discretionary spending on items that add real personal value versus those that only provide superficial value, and choosing which items for personal care and consumption are considered a necessity versus a luxury, there will be either a blessed flow of agreement and consideration or a very harsh divergence in perspective.

Lastly, I want to talk about the flip side of a woman being a gold-digger and another very recent turn of events with women literally taking care of grown men due to a lack of faith that God will send them a man in good financial standing. These men are intentionally not even trying to improve on their financial standing before entering into a serious relationship, because the woman is considered (by implication or express statement) as a "come up" for him. He knows that he can rely on the finances of the woman as the provider and does not even consider trying to provide for their future family in a substantial manner because in his mind, the woman always will carry the brunt of the financial burden to care for herself, him, and the children. You can find evidence of this mindset in a man during the friendship or dating phase as he hints about needing or borrowing money from you. A real man of faith would figure out how to take care of business as he did before he met you, by earning and generating his own income and not relying on a woman.

Again, I am not saying that a woman can't generate more money than a man through her career, business, real estate or other investments, but the financial distance between the two of them should not be too great. They should still be in the same general income bracket, living the same or a very similar quality of life, for the sake of a peaceful relationship that leads to marriage and caring for children.

Financial fruit examination will start with current living arrangement, as previously discussed, and move into gainful employment. The Bible says that if a man doesn't work, he doesn't eat (2 Thessalonians 3:10). The bare minimum for any man you are considering dating is that he has a real job. A real job is not taking gigs here and there or temporary employment that is not leading anywhere. I have heard all kinds of excuses and reasons to get into a serious relationship with an unstable man. Just keep in mind the reason you are dating in the first place. It's not just to hang out and treat him to a good time, but to get to a place of building a life and raising a family together. Job stability matters.

One real life example gave me a very valuable lesson as I grew older and was getting to know men over 40. If a man was new to his career, either interviewing, in training or in his job for less than three years, there was always something else going on beneath the surface. I started to wonder what these men were doing throughout their 20s and 30s to wind up in a new, entry level, labor position in their early or mid-forties. I was in my mid-thirties and had worked my way up the corporate ladder for over 15 years at that point in my life. Therefore, I also made decent income, enough to afford a comfortable quality of life. These men could not carry on the same financial conversations about investing in real estate, stocks or start-ups or career related conversations about the pressures of working in upper-level management, supervising, leading, and mentoring. Most importantly, what was the reason these men were struggling in the workforce at that age? Why hadn't they found their own career path and solid financial footing during early adulthood? Now I am not talking about men who were employed by a big business that had layoffs or one that went out of business leaving them at the point of starting over. That is a different story.

This range of possibilities is why you take time to examine financial fruit of gainful employment. When you look at the root of what the man believes about discipline, work ethic, integrity, and loyalty, you will find either a mature man who can handle the responsibility of providing for a family (and not a short-term provision, but a lasting foundation) or a man who lacks financial and work-related wisdom and skills.

There are other ways to generate income unrelated to job employment which also speaks to fruitfulness in a man's life. If he generates money illegally or unethically, there is a deep-rooted belief system and a lack of spiritual maturity that will cause major problems in his life and possibly your own life in the long run. Moreover, this type of behavior is ungodly and speaks to his level of spiritual immaturity.

I remember I had a conversation with a man who lacked financial stability about an issue I was having in my job. He told me to go in the next day and curse them out. I thought he was joking. I looked in his eyes and he was not joking at all. As a matter of fact, he gave me a full response as to why cursing them out would be justified. I listened, but my mind wandered to a place of now being nervous about this person I was dating. I thought about the fact that he was supposed to be a man of God, but he believed it was okay to curse people out. I thought about the fact that he knew I worked in a professional environment and had a high pay grade, but somehow those facts did not register with him. I thought about how he must have made some impulsive, ungodly and unwise decisions in his career, which is why his career was non-existent and he was always in between jobs.

Also keep in mind that although it is amazing to have big dreams and visions, if a man is not intentionally working towards those dreams and goals, they are what we call pipe dreams. All talk and no action will never pay any bills or send your children to the best Christian private school. Not only will a man on a true mission be able to articulate his vision and what he is working towards, he will be able to detail the active steps he is taking and measurable goals he has set without you leading him towards that vision. If it's a vision from God, the Holy Spirit will lead him.

Here is the balance to this subsection about finances. I hope that as you have read through this section, you have been inspired about what you can do to enhance your financial position as well. Don't hold back on taking your career or business to the next level. God will send you a man who is not intimidated by or trying to use you. Don't wait to invest or purchase a home. Pay down your debt. Build your savings and retirement accounts. Start the business that you are inspired to launch. Go as high as God wants to take you financially and don't be afraid that you will somehow make yourself undesirable. The man God is sending will complement your drive and ambition.

REAL LIFE EXAMPLE

I love giving this real-life example whenever I teach about how a woman can make more money than a man, but still not emasculate him or be used by him as some sort of sugar-mama. I know a woman who is worth millions and her husband is a six-figure earner. They made an agreement when they got married that although she would purchase their new home outright, he would be responsible for all the bills within the home. So even though she paid the mortgage, he provided for the family by taking care of the light, gas and water bills, internet service, lawn care, pool maintenance, house cleaning service, groceries, and other household expenses. He provided for his family, even though she generated a significant amount more money than he did. They made this choice together during this courtship phase of their relationship and their home is peaceful as a result.

OTHER RELATIONSHIPS

It is not enough to consider only your own personal relationship with the man you are dating when it comes to long term commitment. A clear way to ascertain his beliefs and values, especially concerning how he will lead his home, is by examining the fruit of the other diverse relationships in his life.

HIS IMMEDIATE AND EXTENDED FAMILY

Here are some things to consider: *Does he have a good relationship with his parents and siblings? Even if he was not raised by his biological parents, what is his relationship with those who cared for him and taught him about life?*

Most of us were taught about the importance of understanding how well a man treats his mom and sisters as a barometer of how he will treat a woman in a romantic relationship. While it is true that you can get a glimpse of how a man cares for someone he loves, it is not always true that he will treat you that way. After all, do you treat your man-friends the same way you treat your father and brother? No, they are in different categories. As well, you know men that treat their mom and sisters amazingly well, but run through other women like play toys, leaving a trail of broken hearts behind them. I personally know a man who reveres his mother but abuses women he is in relationships with. For this reason, I believe it is important to examine a man's relationship with his family, but also pay attention to how he treats you individually.

Now when it comes to a Spirit-filled man, you can look at how he treats those he loves as something to look forward to once he is truly in love with you. Check out his loyalty, understanding, patience and how he accesses the wisdom of the Holy Spirit in his interactions with those whom he loves when engaged in tough conversations and decision-making. Focus on the fruit of his family relationships. What types of seeds has he sown into those relationships and what is the harvest that he is now living in?

While we are on the topic of family, consider that when the Lord plans to bring two people together in matrimony, he also has a plan for the joining of the two families. This is why, when you study the Bible, you discover the Lord gave strict instructions about who the children of Israel should and should not marry because God had and still has generations on his mind. There is ministry embedded within family dynamics. Right now you might be a significant other, but once you are married, you could be the very messenger of Christ to lead his aunt or sister or cousin to the Lord through your lifestyle and well as your words.

It's also highly important to examine how he is as a father if he already has children, in addition to how he treats and engages with his children's mother or even his ex-wife. It's a shame that in the world we live in, finding a man over 35 with no children or prior marriages is uncommon. But we live in a world (no matter where you are geographically located) that does not have the principles of God as a foundation for societal establishment. You may also be a woman who has made some unsavory choices and is now a single mom waiting on your prince charming. It's true that you will all create your own family dynamic together once you are married, but making sure that both families are a good fit before you give your heart to the man is the wisest decision you can make.

Here are some things to consider: *Is he respectful of his children's mother/ex-wife in a healthy manner? Does their relationship make you feel uncomfortable due to lack of boundaries and emotional ties still present? Do his children enjoy being with their dad and speak highly of him? Does he teach his current children the ways of the Lord and is he a good role model of how to live as a kingdom minded man?*

HIS FRIENDS AND ACQUAINTANCES

Here are some things to consider: *How does he interact with his closest friends and distant acquaintances? Does he have a positive reputation or is he hard to get along with?*

None of us are perfect and we all are striving to be more Christ-like. But even the Proverbs 31 woman's husband had a good reputation of leadership and engaging in a positive way with other leaders in the city (Proverbs 31:23). In order to produce such a good reputation there were seeds of goodness, reliability, integrity, community leadership and good citizenship that were sown over the years. When it comes to identifying a man of God's reputation, look to hear what those close to him (in addition to acquaintances and distant friends) are saying and describing about him.

When it comes to his close friends, not only are you looking for his reputation but also listen to the stories of how their friendship has developed over the years and where they are in present day interactions. If a man has no long-term friendships, not even one, that is a clear indication that he will not make a good friend to you, even before you become relationally committed. You do want to be his best friend at some point, but surely you will not be his one and only friend. To maintain a healthy balance in romantic relationships, each person should still have at least one blessed friendship outside of the relationship.

Also consider how his closest friends react to meeting you the first time or how they treat you when you are all together. I heard a saying when I was younger, that men act just like their best friends when you aren't around. You may have heard the saying "Birds of a feather flock together." That's exactly what this saying means. While these men are not exactly alike, there is a reason they are friends. They enjoy similar entertainment and lifestyles. Otherwise, they wouldn't be close friends; they would have outgrown one another. Therefore, you can catch a glimpse of a man's inner character when you encounter his closest friends.

Think about how he speaks of his friends and engages with them. Is he kind and patient with his friends? Is he controlling and two-faced? Does he love his friends in words and in deed? Does he have a giving heart, or is he self-centered and selfish? Every relationship has its own dynamics, and you will have to use discernment and wisdom in identifying good, deep-rooted fruit or superficial, surface level interactions. Keep in mind that a mature man of God who is filled with and led by the Holy Spirit should have positive and healthy friendships and acquaintances in his life. The

Holy Spirit teaches us how to create blessed (not perfect) relationships.

SERVICE TO GOD

Our priority as believers is to love and serve God, by loving and serving others. While there are many ways to serve God, when considering a man's service to God, it should be clearly evident in his life. His service should also be motivated by and saturated in the love of Christ.

Serving within the church is a clear sign that the Holy Spirit is working on the inside of his spirit. The church has many needs within the house of God and each of us has a role to play in bringing the vision God has given to the local church into fruition.

Think about it like this: if a man is not willing to submit to church leadership, how willing is he to submit to the leadership of the Holy Spirit? If a man is not willing to sacrifice his wants and personal convenience to serve the Body of Christ, how willing will he be in sacrificing his wants and personal convenience to serve his family? If the man is not spiritually mature enough to understand the purpose and desire of God for service within the house of God, is he really spiritually mature enough to love you as Christ loves the church?

Very clear red flags fly when a man does not believe in partnering with a ministry, let alone serving in the ministry. If he does not believe in the covering and leadership of the pastors and ministry leaders, he does not believe in the order that God himself has created. There has always been a church order since the beginning of time, which required the people of God to submit and follow. Yet, there is protection in this order that God has set up. There is provision and purpose locked within submission to this order.

A mature man of God understands that he is not created to operate in spiritual isolation, but that he needs the church and likewise, the church needs him. He has gifts and callings locked up on the inside of his born-again spirit. If he is not sensing or obeying Holy Spirit's nudge to answer the call of God on his life through ministry, this is a sign. He will not be ready to lead and cover a family spiritually if he himself has not yet submitted to such a covering from his own pastor and ministry leaders.

Keep in mind that although examining the fruit of a man's service and submission to God is highly important, it is not the only basis for determining spiritual maturity. There are men at different stages of their spiritual journey who serve in the ministry. Some men may be new believers and although they serve, they have not yet developed enough spiritually to lead a family. Some men may be returning to God after a hard season and are in the midst of spiritual rejuvenation, still not yet ready to cover and lead a family spiritually. Then there are those who are truly wolves in sheep's clothing. They go through the motions of church and godliness but are demonically oppressed and engage in ungodly behavior outside of the church. This is the reason that balance is key to successful fruit examination.

I was in a relationship with a man who was a deacon at his church. He faithfully served and studied his Word. As a matter of fact, one of the things that really made me extremely interested in him was his service to God, serving the homeless in a separate ministry organization outside of church in addition to his normal church duties. I was so impressed that even when I saw blatant signs of carnality and worldliness, I tried to intercede for him as we dated in hopes that his lifestyle behind the scenes would begin to align with the ministry works he participated in. Have you heard the saying, "smoke and mirrors"? That's exactly what was taking place in this relationship. He put on a good show, but when he took his Sunday suit off, he was a weed smoking, cussing, fornicating and lustful manipulator of women. My prayers were not going to change him; only a work of the Holy Spirit within him could cause the radical breakthrough his soul required before he would be ready to be any woman's husband.

Therefore, you must look at the totality of the fruit of the man you are in a relationship with to determine whether he has the good fruit you desire to see within your home and family once the two become one.

RULE #8:

TRUST IN GOD, NOT MAN

Trusting in a man can be tricky at times, but it shouldn't be. God never intended women to be hurt or jaded by failed romantic relationships or broken relationships with male family members. Although I am not a therapist, I understand that the experiences you have with male family members impact your romantic re-lationships as an adult and the experiences you have with significant others. Also those experiences you don't person-ally have, but are a witness to in the lives of those close to you, may cause you to garner trust issues with men.

The tricky part about instilling trust is that your filter of past experiences is valid to a certain extent. There is a time for healing, forgiving, letting go, and moving on; while there is also a time to learn and recognize patterns and red flags that are cues of untrue behavior or feelings.

There is a difference between having trust issues and having sharp discernment. The key to distinguishing exactly what your spirit is communicating with your mind is to identify the birthplace of the problem and message. Are you reading into a situation or the man's behavior based on your experiences, interactions, or past relationships? Or is it true discernment picking up on odd behavior or speech? Rule #4 goes into much more detail about identifying situations in which you have trust issues versus when you are discerning correctly. Right now, I want to help you understand how important it is to put your trust in God during the dating process, not necessarily the man himself.

I have encountered many women who blame God for every failed relationship in their past. They angrily pray and say, "God, how could YOU let this happen?" or "Why did YOU let this man hurt me?" or "Why do YOU keep sending me these trifling men?" As if God is somehow responsible for the actions of a man that hurts you. He is not. Is God responsible for your actions and day to day choices? Or are you an individual who makes your own decisions?

There is a spirit behind everything that takes place in this earthly realm. There are light and dark spirits. People are influenced by spirits, both light and dark, in addition to their own flesh and carnal nature. To blame God for the actions of a person that was influenced either by a dark spirit, or by their own carnal, weak flesh is not fair to a loving Heavenly Father, who only wants what's best for you.

As we go into unveiling the layers of protection God has given us, I want to make it clear that I am not saying that men, in general, are untrustworthy. I am not saying that there is no point in trusting men because they will hurt you. I am not against men. I love men of God who exemplify the love of Christ. I believe there is an abundance of great, high-caliber men, as the kingdom of God is not deficient in any area, including God-fearing men.

Yet, to keep God first and not make a man you're dating an idol of your heart and the sole focus of your attention and energy, it's important to trust in God, not in him (although you will get to the point where you trust him because you trust God).

The love God has for us is real. It is the knowledge, understanding and receipt of this love that will help you to put your trust completely in him while you are dating, without fear of devastation and heartbreak. Practically speaking, it's in God's dynamic protection of us that we can avoid the traps and snares of the enemy early on in the friendship season of dating.

God gives layers of protection well before you make a decision to go all in and give your heart to a man. The issue is that with each layer, you can choose to ignore, disregard, push to the side or otherwise avoid acknowledging anything that should give you pause (or bring the relationship to a screeching halt) in the early stages of getting to know the man.

LAYERS OF PROTECTION

The Word of God

The Holy Scripture gives much guidance, wisdom, and warnings when it comes to how we live our Christian lives, to include engaging in romantic relationships. This means everything from abstaining from sex until marriage and understanding what the works of the flesh are, to what becomes of those who operate in their flesh with no repentance, and providing clear instructions not to join ourselves together with non-believers. All these instructions are found within the Bible. When you choose to operate outside of the protection of the written Word of God, you also open yourself up to experience heartbreak, devastation and wasted time, effort and energy with the wrong man.

Prayer & Hearing God's Voice

Each believer of Christ Jesus should spend regular time in prayer and be able to easily discern the voice of God. Jesus Christ said, "My sheep hear my voice..." (John 10:27), which means that every Christian should in fact hear the voice of God. We should be so acquainted with the Holy Spirit because we spend time in prayer, study, and worship that there is little to no confusion when God speaks to us. Unfortunately, many women don't know the voice of God for themselves and are often confused about when the Lord is speaking to them or if it's their own thoughts. They fail to realize that the fiery darts of the enemy are also "thoughts" that spring forth in the mind. This layer of protection is vital during the dating process because the Lord has much to say to you about someone you are considering opening up and giving your heart to.

A Discerning Spirit

When you are born again, the Holy Spirit will begin to

communicate directly with your spirit, since you are now joined together with Christ and the Holy Spirit lives on the inside of you. This communication is not the gift of discerning of spirits described in 1 Corinthians 12:10 (which is given to identify and cast out demon spirits for deliverance), but a personal unction within that lets you know something is not quite right. The world calls this type of discerning "woman's intuition." At times you may not be able to put into words what your spirit is picking up, yet this nudge shouldn't be ignored. God's Spirit on the inside of you wants you to be aware that something is not right. Likewise, it is this same experience that will give you great peace and calm when God is giving you the green light to rest and trust him in the process when all is well.

Spiritual Teachers and Leaders

Recent years have produced an abundance of Christian women being hurt or deceived at church and unfortunately, this has caused women of God to lose trust in the church and bible teachers, preachers, and leaders. Of course, I don't have the statistical data to compare the loss of church members and personal trust in true Christian ministries, but it is imperative that this layer of protection not be lost or forgotten. God has placed spiritual gifts within the Body of Christ for a reason. Teachers make the Word of God practical and understandable for daily application. Pastors cover their local congregation with love, compassion, and leadership to maintain order, consistency, and unity among believers in a geographic location. Even lay ministers can encourage or rebuke with the goal of helping you to stay on track with God and make wise, blessed choices concerning the man you are dating.

Godly Examples of Others

Apostle Paul encouraged believers to imitate him as he imitates Christ (1 Corinthians 11:1). When we see others who have truly followed God and submitted to the uncompromised Word of God in their love life, we can follow their lead and use them as an example of love, dating, and godly relationships. There are seasons when you will be exposed to these types of beautiful, joyful, loving, and godly relationships. They will appear almost perfect with two Christians appearing to live in marital bliss. The Lord is not revealing these relationships to make comparisons or to make you feel bad that it hasn't happened for you yet, but quite the opposite. He intends for this exposure to build your faith, increase your expectation, and motivate you to persevere, believing that God's very best for you is still out there and that he will join you together with your "perfect" love in perfect timing. These godly examples provide a layer of protection for you in that God is showing you what his love truly looks like in a God-glorifying marriage that exemplifies the description given in Ephesians Chapter 5.

Family and Friends

There are many times when God will use your family and friends to speak a word of wisdom, encouragement and/or warning to you during the single season. At times, it may come from the most unlikely of sources, but it is the vessel before you in that present moment whom God chooses to use because you will listen to them. You will hear them. This does not mean that every word of advice given from your family and friends is from God. You are still required to employ discernment and ensure that the Holy Spirit is speaking to you and it's not that person's flesh or a dark spirit speaking through them. When it comes to your parents, their love for you is typically so pure, you can trust that they have your best interest at heart with no ulterior motive and therefore, heavenly protection is embedded in the words they share concerning your singleness or the person who you are dating. Again, this is not a blanket statement, as there are some abusive and unloving parents in the world, but most often, the parental perspective is a layer of protection from God. If you have friends in your life that you believe are covenant friendships (brought together by God for his plans, purposes, and intentions), those conversations can also be used as valuable streams of protective reasoning, observance, and wisdom.

Blatant Red Flags and Warnings

The Bible teaches us in Luke 8:17 that all secrets are revealed, and hidden things are brought into the light. This scripture is not meant to instill fear in us, but instead to bring us peace in knowing that God will ensure we are not totally deceived in any situation. When you are building a friendship with a new man-friend, it can be hard to pick up on subtle clues that he is not in the one from God when you are having a good time and your rose-colored-lenses are on. The excitement of new opportunities and the prospect of male attention, companionship, answered prayers and the possibilities of love can cloud judgment. In these moments, God will give blatant red flags and warnings (if needed) before you get too deep into the relationship. How many times have you thought to yourself "I should have known..." because of an obvious sign that you chose to ignore or attempted to pray through? In the end, your lack of acknowledgement of these signs ended up biting you in the butt. God will surely give the signs we pray for in relationships. These signs will be plain, and they will be clear because this is a layer of protection God provides to his daughters.

Now that we have gone through six different layers of protection, you can see why it is important to both maintain your relationship with God, rest in his protection, and trust in God, not man.

I have counseled many women of God that claim they had no idea a certain man would hurt them. However, after discussing each layer of protection and probing deeper, they would admit that the signs and warnings were evident early on.

Keep in mind that just as God will protect you from danger, as you trust in him to send your prince charming, he will also provide great confirmation when he has arrived. Jaded by hurt, and bitter from disappointment, women have claimed that trusting God to send you a true, pure love that exceeds your prayers and expectations is unrealistic. I encourage you to place your faith in God and not the experiences of others. According to Ephesians 3:20 (one of my favorite scriptures to stand on concerning standards and qualities in the man you pray for), God can and will exceed abundantly our highest prayers, hopes, and dreams in any area of our lives where the power of God is at work on the inside of us. If you feed your spirit with faith, the power of God is at work on the inside of you. If you renew your mind with the Word of God concerning your singleness and desire for marriage, the power of God is at work on the inside of you.

Again, I reiterate, you focus on trusting God and as the Lord begins to reveal the inner character and heart of the man you are dating, you can trust him because God has given you the green light to do so. If you focus on trusting God first and not trusting the man first and then asking God whether you can continue to trust him, allow the layers of protection to bring confirmation and revelation so that you can begin trusting the man because you first trusted God. You will experience greater peace if you follow this order of trust.

RULE #9:

ENSURE YOUR VISION IS IN ALIGNMENT

Your vision for multiple aspects of your life must be in alignment with the man of God's vision for his own life. Newlyweds who do not discuss and share visions prior to marriage are in for a rude awakening.

When you combine Habakuk 2:2-3 and Amos 3:3, the foundation for this biblical rule for godly dating is formed:

Habakkuk 2:2-3 (NKJV)
Then the Lord answered me and said:
"Write the vision
And make it plain on tablets,
That he may run who reads it.
For the vision is yet for
an appointed time;
But at the end it will speak,
and it will not lie.
Though it tarries, wait for it;
Because it will surely come,
It will not tarry.

Amos 3:3 (NKJV)
Can two walk together,
unless they are agreed?

Once you are married, you and your husband will need to be in agreement, on one accord, in order to flow in unity and harmony within the home. The vision that you both have for yourselves as individuals, as well as the vision you both share for the family will come into play in many diverse situations. Keep in mind, you're supposed to run with the vision, steadily working towards bringing the dream alive. How can you run with a vision if you don't agree on what exactly that vision is?

Before you even consider God's vision for your future marriage and family, early in the friendship season, you must examine the personal vision you each have for your own lives. Here are some questions to keep in mind:

♡ Where do you see yourself in 10 years and where does he see himself in 10 years?

♡ What are each of your spiritual and ministry goals?

♡ What type of family goals do you both have for within the home? What about your extended family?

♡ How do you want your lifestyle to grow/change/shift over the next 10-20 years?

♡ What quality of life are you working towards now and hoping to enter into in the near or distant future?

♡ How are you both working on growing as people, leaders, professionals, ministers, citizens, givers/ philanthropists, business owners, etc. and what personal and professional goals have you each set to grow in these areas?

♡ What are some health and fitness goals you are both striving towards?

♡ When it comes to earning money, sowing, giving, investing, and spending, do you both have a personal vision for your finances now as singles, and how will this vision change once you combine households after marriage?

These questions may seem a bit intense, but you will not tackle these conversations on the first or even the second date. As you are growing closer and getting to know each other, you will get a clear picture of each of your visions and see if they are similar or drastically different.

Keep in mind that a mature man of God has a vision for his life in each of these areas and in much more detail. Vague responses or thoughts such as "I just want to be happy," "I want my children to go to college," and "I want my business to be successful," are not visions because there are no concrete goals attached to them. They are simply vague wants or desires. There is a difference.

A vision is tangible and attainable. You attach measurable goals to a vision, and you can pinpoint exactly where someone is on the path towards bringing their vision into fruition. You also want to listen for the will of God, leadership of the Holy Spirit and plans of God embedded within your life's vision. A Romans 8:14 man of God would not make any plans that are not birthed from the Spirit and governed by his Heavenly Father. This is true of a Romans 8:14 woman of God as well.

It is not enough simply to get on board with a man's plans and submit to his vision without having gotten clear about God's will for your own life first. How many married women have you heard of complain that they have lost themselves in marriage and motherhood? This notion stems from not being fully clear about who they were as a single woman and letting their relationship lead their life, instead of letting God lead them. This is dangerous. You don't want to sacrifice your calling, anointing, or even your way of life because you give your heart to a man with a mismatched vision or no vision at all. Not only will you be unable to agree on anything, but you will be unable to run with the vision God has for your life.

MODERN DAY/ REAL LIFE ISSUES

WHEN YOU DON'T AGREE...

During one very rough season of my life, I was involved with a man who already had two children from a prior relationship (not marriage) and still had an ungodly soul tie with the woman, although he claimed to have moved on. Throughout our relationship we had many intense arguments about his interactions and future plans with his ex. We disagreed on what was appropriate behavior for a co-parenting relationship when one party is in a committed relationship with someone else. We argued about how personally and intimately involved with her life he should be since they were not in a relationship anymore yet needed to raise children together.

I didn't believe he should spend the night at her home for a couple of days just to help out with the children. I didn't agree that he should have daily conversations with her on the phone discussing personal things that had nothing to do with the children. I did not agree that he should be responsible for taking care of her financial needs in the future, providing for her as a woman, if he intended to have a future and family with me. It appeared as if he wanted to have two families, and I was totally uncomfortable and not on board with those choices. After speaking with his mother who believed that all of his actions were reasonable and even expected because of his culture and childhood experiences, I wondered how we could ever move forward in peace.

I prayed and Amos 3:3 continually rose up in my spirit. How could we ever stop arguing and walk together in peace if we don't agree on this estranged, yet very present relationship with his child's mother? I certainly didn't expect him to never speak to her or even hold any grudges against her. I wanted them both to be happy individuals, happy parents and simply live separate lives so they each could move on, especially him as the one I was attempting to grow a new relationship with. I needed him to sever the emotional, mental and physical ties from her, but he refused. He explained how he felt his actions were necessary and then proceeded to explain how he planned to provide for her in the future, based on a few promises he made years before when they were together.

It was all too much and completely unbiblical. God intends for a man to leave his mother and father and cleave to his wife. God does not intend for a man to cleave to his children's mother and his wife at the same time. Polygamy can take many forms and I refused to be a member of a two-family situation. Since he refused to simply focus on the children and provide for them, be an amazing father and be a kind ex to his children's mother, it was clear that we could never walk in agreement. We had two different visions for our future, and he needed a woman who was on board with his ongoing, very personal relationship with his children's mother.

Here are some signs that may be present in your relationship when you don't agree on certain topics and will struggle to walk together towards shared vision as a couple:

- Arguing over the same issue repeatedly

- Verbal agreement but no corresponding behavioral changes

- Long term goals/visions seem to be set in stone with no room for flexible consideration

- Hiding or withholding information for fear of being misunderstood by the other person

WHEN HE HAS NO PERSONAL SPIRITUAL VISION FOR HIMSELF...

In another season I was with a man who I believed had a personal spiritual vision for himself and could have a vision of raising my son as his own (once our relationship became serious), but soon found out that both assumptions on my part were incorrect.

When we met, he told me his story of his personal salvation through Christ, a beautiful moment where he had reached rock bottom and cried out to God from a place of brokenness and desperation. God heard and answered him, and he was moved by a powerful, tangible presence of God in the privacy of his own home. He knew God had saved his soul in that moment and decided to seek God more passionately. This wonderful event took place less than a year prior to our meeting. When we connected, he had only been saved in accordance with Romans 10:9-10 less than a year and was moving along slowly with studying, understanding and applying the Word of God to his life. Additionally, he found that he lacked a Word of Faith, Bible teaching ministry in his small town, so he continued to attend his local church, which did not allow for significant spiritual growth, although he was aware he needed it.

At this point in time, I had also experienced a supernatural encounter with the Holy Spirit 10 years before and had lived a zealous Christian lifestyle of ministry, calling, preaching, teaching, and prophesying ever since. Not only did I have the blessing of learning the things of God and real-life application of the scriptures from the Word of Faith, teaching ministry I attended, but I knew the plan of God. My personality, background and calling all played a part in my own spiritual growth and acceleration into ministry.

Although my new male friend had grown up in church, he had yet to experience God and grow with the Holy Spirit as I had done over the past decade. You see, growing up in church is not the same as having a real, intimate relationship with the Holy Spirit and growing in love with Him. Reading scriptures is not the same as understanding, interpreting, and teaching others unto spiritual revelation. Attending a church service is not the same as presenting true worship and honor to God while allowing his spirit to minister to your spirit personally. Personal conviction is not the same as feeling guilty, yet it is through this conviction and being led as you practice the presence of God unto obedience that you begin to experience true spiritual growth and increased personal and corporate anointing. This personal conviction was missing in the life of this older gentleman I was dating and likewise there were certain lifestyle choices and behaviors in both of our lives that did not align. This is a huge issue, although many women in similar situations determine that it is no big deal when you are not on the same page spiritually with the man you are dating.

While it is not meant for us to judge anyone in an unrighteous manner or compare one person's salvation to another's, we can judge a tree by its fruit (Matthew 7:16–20), especially when it concerns the spiritual maturity of the man we are dating. God is maturing each of us spiritually at different levels based on our comprehension, exposure and willingness to obey his leadership.

The personal maturation we each experience with God gives light to the personal spiritual vision we have for ourselves. A woman with a personal spiritual vision sees herself going higher in the things of God, growing closer to the Lord in many ways. She sees herself strengthening her discernment, understanding more of her calling and anointing, repenting from covert and hidden sins, teaching and raising up more disciples of Christ, and ultimately becoming more and more Christ-like, day by day, moment by moment. The same is true for a man of God who has a personal spiritual vision for himself. He sees himself becoming more of the mighty man of valor the Lord created him to be. Not only does he see himself not remaining stagnant spiritually, but he is actively pursuing spiritual growth which is evident in his words and deeds. He had a spiritual vision for his own life before meeting you and the vision is established without your assistance. You do not need to help him see who he is in God, because the Holy Spirit is actively working in and through him.

What if this is not true of the man you are considering as you read through this chapter? Think about how your spiritual differences will create varying visions and lack of agreement in the relationship while you're dating, as well as long-term once you are married. Consider what will take place when you have strong spiritual convictions based on lessons God has taught you over the years that he himself has not yet learned. He will not believe on the same level as you do and his expectations of what is and is not appropriate as two Christian singles will create tension in the relationship.

At the onset of one particular relationship, I was in the middle of going to the next level concerning my life's purpose, calling, ministry and spiritual gifts. I was reaching thousands of women around the world with the message of celibacy and holiness as single women, helping women create lifestyles of fasting, prayer and understanding prophetic messages in addition to helping women break soul ties, heal from brokenness, and begin living whole and fulfilled lives as single God-fearing women. He, on the other hand, did not even have a full understanding of what spiritual gifts, anointing and calling were, let alone what his specific life purpose was. When I initiated a conversation about understanding his life's purpose by seeking God in study and prayer, it ended on a positive note, but still with disparities. I had hoped that he would have been intrigued enough to start seeking God on his own about his purpose, anointing and calling. I wanted our conversation to spark a flame in his spirit that would begin a beautiful journey of purpose discovery and hopefully our callings would come into alignment. Yet, after this conversation, it never came up again, nor did he begin to pursue God any more intentionally than before, in any area of his life, including his life's purpose.

He did not have a vision for himself to grow spiritually in the specific direction that I was growing, which was okay in the end. He made it clear that he was on a journey to start reading the Bible more consistently, while I was on a journey of holding regular prayer meetings and beginning to prophesy to nations. There was nothing wrong with either of our journeys; they were just different and not cohesive. I understood what the bible teaches in Ephesians 5 about the husband being the spiritual head of the home and desired nothing less than God's standard in my marriage. I knew God had a spiritually strong husband in mind for me, one who could teach and cover me as Christ does for his church. After all, our marriages are supposed to be reflections of Christ's love for his church. Therefore, even though we weren't even close to discussing marriage yet, it was evident early on that the spiritual distance between us was too great and we would not be able to walk in agreement or even create a shared vision for our lives together.

Here are some signs to look for during the friendship phase of a relationship when you are just getting to know each other, to determine whether your personal spiritual visions are in alignment or not:

♡ You live different Christian lifestyles. One of you believes it's okay to fornicate, the other is celibate. One of you believes it is okay to drink, smoke and party, the other does not. One of you believes it is okay to use profanity or live in poverty, the other does not.

♡ You see yourself in different places spiritually five years from now. One of you sees yourself starting a ministry or launching a marketplace business, the other not only doesn't see you doing any of those things, but they don't see themselves fitting in with that type of life.

♡ You have a different foundation of faith altogether. One of you believes in hearing from God regularly, practicing the presence of God and praying in tongues (personal prayer language and baptism of the Holy Spirit) while the other does not believe any of those things and is content never discerning the voice of God or praying in tongues.

♡ The man may say that he has faith and believes the same way as you do, but you don't see any forward movement or actual evidence of his personal relationship with God and personal spiritual vision.

HIGHLIGHT THIS: You cannot help a man by creating a spiritual vision for him and then trying to get him on board with the potential of the man you believe he could be. You must trust that God will bring you together with your future husband after levels of potential have been fulfilled. You must be able to accept him as he is and then look forward to him becoming an even better man and Christian. No matter how much you pray for him or try to influence him with your godly lifestyle, you cannot accelerate the rate of growth he will experience with the Holy Spirit. HIs personal spiritual growth is between him and God. If you attempt to stay with him and become his spiritual covering and pastor, you literally are attempting to reverse the roles God created in Ephesians Chapter 5. You will only end up distracting him, while he is also distracting you from ultimate purpose fulfillment.

Further, don't be fooled by stories of other women who claimed to have met and married a spiritually immature man who later became extremely godly. These women were probably at the same spiritual level of these men when they met. Certainly God can provide a man with whom we are equally yoked. If indeed the woman still claims that she was on a higher spiritual level than her husband and married him anyway, understand that this situation is unbiblical and not how God intended us to come together in relationships. Scripture after scripture passage and many bible stories reveal the heart of God concerning marriages and the spiritual maturity required of the husband.

WHEN HE HAS NO VISION OF BEING A FATHER TO YOUR CHILDREN...

During the same aforementioned relationship, I also discovered through discernment and many unanswered questions that this man of God did not have a vision of being father to my child. He also did not have a vision of having any additional children. I found that quite interesting given that I was a younger woman and he made it clear that he enjoyed being in relationships with younger women as opposed to women in his own age bracket. He was only nine years older than I was but was close to 50. Since he had raised 3 children from his previous marriage and another relationship, with his youngest child being in her teen years, he described a vision he had of soon becoming a grandfather. He told me he was looking forward to becoming a grandfather soon. That was the vision he had for himself.

I, on the other hand, had a young child and a strong desire to have a few more children once I was married. My vision for my future marriage was one of raising a young family and his vision was of entering another generation of caring for grown children and spoiling grandkids.

Another painful realization was how he interacted or lacked interaction with my child once we began discussing the future and our relationship became serious. While I did not expect him to step into a fatherhood role at that point of the relationship (it was serious but not that serious), I did expect him to be considerate of my child and acknowledge he was a priority in my life. Sadly, this was not the case. He acted as if his needs should come before those of my child and as if he was non-existent at times. I know firsthand how it feels to be the child that is tolerated, but not truly desired or loved and I never want my child to experience that type of father figure.

The man God sends will have a vision for your relationship and at some point, will also have one that includes all the children involved with your union. He has to see himself as a "bonus" dad to your child/children and not as if you are the grand prize and your children are insignificant. A true man of God will begin to hear from the Lord as you grow closer in your relationship about the impact he will make, even as it concerns the children's spiritual growth. After all, he is to lead the family spiritually and this includes teaching and being an amazing example of godliness for the children.

As a mother, you will be able to discern and quickly pick up clues if the man has this vision for your current/future children or not. God reveals all things and is very concerned about the little innocent children who need us to take care of them. You will know the difference between a man being polite and kind just to get on your good side, versus his intentions towards your children being pure and sincere. The most important thing to remember is no matter how good a man he is to you, never put your children last or falsely believe that if the man is good to you, he will be good to your children.

Many children have been neglected, abused, and molested because women have chosen to focus only on how the man treats them and they pay no attention to whether he has a vision for being a good father to her children. Just because the biological father is a good role model and teacher, does not absolve your future husband from responsibility. Remember that children need love and leadership. They need a caring, supportive, and fair father figure in the home who will teach them how to be good individuals and Christians. They need to both feel and truly be cared for and loved by the man you are considering sharing your life with. Prayerfully, their biological father is good to them but the man they will be living with and watching day to day interact with the family is also extremely important.

Here are a few signs that the man you are dating does not have a vision of godly fatherhood for your current/future children:

- When the children's needs are made evident as you are spending time together, he ignores or disregards them.

- If there is a moment when you have to choose between serving his needs or taking care of the children, he prefers and makes clear that he wants you to satisfy or take care of him first, without regard for the child/children.

- He never mentions or inquires about your children when you are growing closer and spending more time together.

- He does not mention having any (more) children or plainly states that he does not want any.

- He barely speaks of his own children or speaks of them with disdain or annoyance.

- He never mentions or brings up what it would be like once your lives are blended, and he is the "bonus" dad.

There will be a good time during the relationship to discuss this very significant issue, but it's definitely not a first date conversation. Yet, especially as you become older, it is increasingly important to have the conversation about children and get a clear picture of what role he is willing to play in the lives of your current/future children. Keep in mind that God is an Ephesians 3:20 God. He will do exceedingly above all you ask, think or imagine, and that includes sending an amazing man that will treat you like the queen that you are, taking blessed care of all the children within the household.

RULE #10:

MAKE ROOM FOR LOVE

This is a very busy world that we live in. At times, it feels as if everything around us is moving in a whirlwind. We race to get up and get ready in the morning, speed down the road to work, rush back home at the end of a long work day (or to pick up the kids, then home), make dinner, give baths, rush to bed and try to also find time for working out, self-care, family time and taking breaks. Let's not even talk about the hectic schedule you have if you are serving in the ministry, running a side business, or writing a new book! Our lives are busy and they are full.

Your life can be full of ministry and service if you are busy giving time and effort at your local church. You could be entrepreneurial or a visionary who spends a lot of time serving and giving in your non-profit or business or pursuing other creative endeavors. If you are a single mom, your life is filled with taking care of your children and keeping them healthy and happy. Those who are close to family live a life full of being there for everyone, taking care of relatives or being a regular support system for those who need it. If your job, career, or business is demanding, your days are full of work, creating, training, teaching, leading, rushed meals and quick snacks on the go, meetings, overtime and late nights working, building and launching.

In addition to your life being full of work, service and personal activities, you also can have a full and even cluttered soul, heart, mind, and spirit. This type of fullness is evident in various ways:

- A cluttered soul is evident when there are unaddressed soul ties that need to be broken.

SCAN ME

Watch the Breaking Toxic Soul Ties Video to see what the Bible teaches about healthy vs. toxic soul ties.

- A cluttered heart is filled with pain, hurt and/or idols that have replaced the space reserved for God.

- A cluttered mind is busy and overwhelmed, never seeming to stop or calm down without the use of self or prescribed medication.

- A cluttered spirit contains beliefs, strongholds or even demonic spirits that require tearing down and even spiritual deliverance.

THINK ABOUT THIS: How would a new, amazing man fit into your full and busy world? Would he blend in seamlessly or would the busyness and clutter of your world cause him to feel unwanted or incompatible? Would the total package of the woman you are and your lifestyle, behaviors and activities bring peace and happiness to the high caliber man of God you are praying for, or would he run for the hills? Are you aware of any "issues" or "baggage" that you know you need to work on but have been avoiding?

I have worked with many women who desired marriage but truly did not have room for the type of man they were praying for to come into their life. If he did show up, they would either not have time for him, drive him away or hurt him deeply because of their natural and spiritual clutter. Maybe you can relate to these women. Do you have a relationship in mind in which you believe the man was truly husband material for you, but you messed up to the point that he left and you could never repair the relationship? We used to call this scenario "the one that got away." If you refer to the bulleted list above, I am sure you could pinpoint an area of your life back then which was cluttered and did not allow room for true love.

MAKING & TAKING TIME FOR LOVE

Part of working on yourself and preparing for the man you are praying for, is getting your life organized into a graceful flow. It doesn't make sense to stop living a full life (in fact I teach quite the opposite), but you should consider how you will make room for love when it arrives.

There was one relationship I was involved in when it was painfully obvious our lives were not going to fit together. I was (and still am) a very busy woman, living a life of purpose, service and realizing ambitious dreams and goals. The man I was dating however, required lots of my time and in fact, consumed more and more of my time. The relationship bordered on co-dependency and I felt drained. I was unable to remain focused on the things of God. It was clear that he was a distraction, as the time spent with him did not encourage or support my endeavors but prevented me from reaching goals prayerfully set before we met. My time with God suffered. My time working in my ministry and calling suffered. Even the time I had set aside for spending with my child slowly diminished as his demands on my time and energy increased. I learned a very valuable lesson in that season that growing closer to a man you are in a relationship with should not cause you to lose yourself or pursuit of God-given goals in the process.

In another season I was involved with a man who lived a very full life (although not as full as mine). He was occupied with his own blessed living and was very understanding of my work, motherhood and self-care needs. We were able to get to know each other peacefully without either of us sacrificing our personal or professional goals. We did not have to talk on the phone for hours a day, although we did speak daily. When we both had a longer slot of free time, we could have deeper conversations. He was not demanding of my time, yet he made it clear that he was into me. It was important to him that we spoke daily for example, even though we might chat only a few moments. Although that relationship had bigger issues, which is why it didn't work out, I can appreciate how we both made room for each other, and our lives flowed well together.

We must have balance when it comes to our service, work, parenting, self-care and other areas of our lives which make a demand on our time. We don't want to make someone we are interested in feel as if we don't have time for them. We each make time for whatever is important to us. It is true however, that when your life is already pretty full, you have to take time from one area to give it to the new man in your life. But we must always remember to keep as priorities the most important things, such as time with God, your children (if you have them) and your health.

Let's discuss the other areas mentioned previously, which you may need to de-clutter to make room for love.

DECLUTTERING

Your soul is composed of your mind, will, emotions, imagination and intellect. Although you could separate each area (and we will delve into a few independently), I want to focus on decluttering your soul as a whole. When your soul is cluttered, it means you have an ungodly soul tie. A soul tie is a special bond God created for a husband and wife, an adjoining of two souls to run one household with one vision and one mind, the mind of Christ. Because this bond was created by God when he brought two people together, his intention was for godly soul ties to last forever. The problem comes in when two single people enter into an ungodly soul tie and struggle to sever ties.

When your soul is cluttered with an ungodly soul tie, it will be very evident in your new relationship. The new man friend may not know how to identify a soul tie, but he will use words such as "baggage" or say you have "issues" when problems arise not relating to the current relationship, but that pertain entirely to a prior relationship or heartbreak. When you have an ex that is very much a part of your emotions and mind, it will be obvious and lead to problems in your new relationship. It may or may not be that you're still in love with your ex. It could be that you haven't fully healed, let go or forgiven them (or yourself) for negative experiences that transpired while you were together. Whether the soul tie is based on positive or negative spiritual entanglement, the tie must be severed and broken permanently so that your soul may effectively be decluttered.

Now, let's talk more about your heart, mind and spirit. We have been told plainly to love the Lord God with all our heart, soul, mind, and strength. Indeed, there is a special place in each of our hearts that is reserved exclusively for God himself. When something else takes root in our hearts in that place reserved for God, it is called an idol.

You see, when God is on the throne of our hearts there is plenty of room for love to flow. Love flows in, love flows out. As our hearts are filled until overflowing with God's love, it is easy to share the right kind of godly love with a man. God's kind of love is not merely an emotional exchange. It certainly is not limited to physical interactions either. God's love is unconditional, unbridled and unlimited. With this type of all-encompassing love moving through your innermost being, your future husband will be blessed beyond measure by your presence in his life.

On the other hand, what if God is not on the throne of your heart? What if certain idols have taken residence in your heart? Examples of idols include the love of money, selfishness or even marriage itself; or the condition that your heart's still broken, filled with hurt and pain not only from relationships but also from childhood or adulthood trauma.

I knew a woman named Clarice who was a clear example of what it looked like to get involved with men when she refused to go through the process to declutter her soul, heart, mind and spirit. She had soul ties to her ex, Sam, a man she was still obviously in love with, yet they hadn't been in a committed relationship in over a decade. The soul tie was obvious since he was in a new relationship (3 or 4 times over) yet would drop everything to answer Clarice's calls and run to her side at any time she needed him. The fact that he had broken her heart and hurt her feelings repeatedly over the years did not change the deep affection she had for him or at times her misguided hope that they would somehow end up together, even though he had children with a few new women in his life, and even had a woman living with him in one season. Clarice thought of and mentioned Sam daily, even when she was in new relationships with other men. These men not only felt uncomfortable because of her closeness to Sam, but the unaddressed brokenness from their relationship would spill over into new relationships. The hurt and pain Sam took Clarice through now made her question the loyalty, faithfulness and sincerity of any new man in her future relationships.

Additionally, because of the clutter in her mind—strongholds she had built up about love and dating—she would unintentionally sabotage new love that came into her life. She was aware of this self-sabotaging behavior but was extremely stuck in her mind and spirit and could not change her ways, thoughts and behaviors, so she concluded time and time again that the men were the problem. I also was aware that there were other deep rooted and unresolved issues pertaining to Clarice's relationship with her parents that resulted in her inability to understand and receive God's love and recognize the difference between love and lust. She wore a mask of confidence but beneath the surface was low self-esteem and a lack of true self-worth.

During your single season, you must do the work to fully declutter any area of your life that may be preventing you from manifesting the true love you pray for. If God did send the man of your dreams today, would you scare him off like Clarice, due to unresolved issues as a result of having a cluttered life? Or, would your true love find a place of rest and peace in you being a part of his life?

SIMPLE STEPS TO DECLUTTERING

Step 1 - Be honest with yourself about where you are spiritually, mentally, and soulfully. In the presence of God is the safest place to be vulnerable. He can help you when you fully open up and trust in him.

Step 2 - Determine what your specific needs are in order to declutter. Do you need deliverance to rid your spirit of demonic ties? Do you need to seek counseling or therapy to heal from and let go of past hurts, pains and traumas?

Do you need to repent from having marriage as an idol and make a firm decision not to do anything to get or keep a man, but rather to be willing to do anything please God?

Step 3 – Make a bold step forward with radical change. Find the right therapist and commit to regular meetings. Start fasting and praying and don't stop until you reach a place of spiritual breakthrough. Do a deep biblical study into the area where you know you have built up a stronghold, so that you can replace that belief with what the Word of God teaches on the matter.

When you follow these steps through to completion you will begin to feel lighter. That is a sign of your life being decluttered. Your mind will start thinking more clearly and you should be able to hear from God better as well. You need a clear spirit, soul and mind to discern God's voice with great clarity. It's just like when you declutter a space, physically speaking. A cluttered room is messy and unorganized, and you can't find anything. You don't invite people over because it is embarrassing. You wouldn't bring a man you really like into a cluttered, filthy room and tell him to "make himself at home." He would run for the hills and find himself a clean woman.

This is not at all to say that you must be perfectly ordered and have yourself 100% together before love finds you. We are all a work in progress. Yet you should have made strides with God decluttering your life before your prince charming finds you, so that when you meet you can focus on growing a blessed friendship, then relationship. If an ex, past pains, soul ties or unresolved childhood issues are present, those things will get in the way of what God wants to do in your life when he sends this amazing blessing your way.

RULE #11:

GUARD YOUR HEART, FOR A SEASON

Have you ever been guilty of moving too fast too soon in a relationship? You were very comfortable with your new man friend and having so much fun getting to know him that you decided to open up your heart very early on in the friendship. You share intimate secrets and private confessions with him. You give him all your trust right away before he even shows you that he can be trustworthy. Your feelings are entangled quickly and the next thing you know, your heart is in his hands so quickly, and you're not even sure how it got there.

If you're anything like me, you're a hopeless romantic. You believe the best in people until they reveal otherwise, and you are very trusting and patient. You desire marriage and are very hopeful with each new rendezvous that this indeed might be the one for you. It's actually easier for you to open up to someone than it is to stay guarded, because you crave that trusting, safe space of companionship.

On the other hand, you could be a woman who has been hardened by disappointment and struggles with emotional availability. You date in hopes of finding love, yet it is extremely difficult to open up and let anyone close to your heart for fear of being tricked, deceived or hurt again. You may have witnessed failed relationships in those close to you and decided to be extremely cautious so that their story doesn't become yours.

Neither of these extremes are the way God intends for us to operate in new relationships. Proverbs 4:23 teaches us to guard our hearts with all vigilance for out of it flows the springs of life. The wisdom of God requires balance in the dating season. Your heart should not be hardened by life, but it also should not be left unguarded. You should keep your heart guarded, but only for a season.

Wisdom is not wearing your heart on your sleeve and revealing all your innermost desires, hopes, dreams or experiences on the first, second or third date. Wisdom is also not being so closed off that the man does not feel as if you want or desire him at all, or that you're closed off to love and new experiences with him. Wisdom is guarding your heart just enough in the beginning stages of friendship and gracefully flowing with the Spirit of God while taking cues from your new friend about when and how to begin lowering your guard.

These two factors will work together in unison. The Lord desires to lead and guide us in every area of our lives, especially matters of the heart. When it is safe to begin letting your guard down, he will give clear signs and confirmations that the man you are dating is trustworthy and honest. He will make it crystal clear that the man offers a safe space for you to open up, share and give more of yourself to as your relationship grows. Likewise, the Holy Spirit will put a pause in your spirit if you are about to give too much of yourself too early on.

You must allow the man of God to prove himself (and this goes both ways) not because you have trust issues with men, but because you are a woman of wisdom allowing your relationship to progress at a smart pace.

I learned this lesson the hard way when I was dating a deacon and gave too much of myself too soon, despite the spiritual leadership the Holy Spirit was providing to me initially. On the first date with this man, the Lord gave me a vision and I was able to see the emotional and mental state he was in beneath the surface. He was a broken, hurting and lonely man, yet he would never admit to that fact. Instead, he said all the right words followed by the perfect corresponding actions giving the appearance of true love and focused commitment to me and only me. There was a great disparity between what God had shown me and what his words and actions were speaking to my emotions. I chose to follow my heart (which was completely on my sleeve), pray about the vision I had on the first date and move forward into a deeper, more intimate relationship with him. I hoped for the best and decided that maybe God had given me the vision because I was the one that was supposed to love him patiently to wholeness. This is what I call self-deceit, which was a huge mistake. Time revealed that my vision was accurate as his true feelings and beliefs surfaced through words and actions that started becoming contradictory, broken promises, withholding of information, sneaky behavior and a sharp pulling away after he got the things he wanted from me, yes, even physically.

I was so upset with myself and emotionally devastated. Even though I knew that I disregarded what God was showing me for protection and made a choice to press forward led by my own emotions and what sounded nice, I was still hurt. My heart was fully exposed, but so was my mindset and beliefs about trusting God.

SCAN ME

Watch this video where I teach what true love is biblically speaking.

The Lord wants to protect his daughters from heartbreak and deception. His will is for us to experience pure and true love, not emotional devastation. He will give you clear warning signs and red flags, in addition to the biblical standards he has laid out, to provide almost instantaneous protection.

In addition to spiritual protection from God, you also want to observe the man's actions, try not to read too much into a kind gesture, and allow some time for trustworthiness to be established. When the deacon and I first began dating, I allowed all of his kind gestures and perfect diction to sway me closer and closer to him emotionally, even when his emotions were still hidden away. But I couldn't tell. I was so caught up in my own emotions. Also, because he checked off almost every box of answered prayer and was in tune with meeting my needs, it was very easy to let my guard down quickly. For example, what woman doesn't want to hear, "I've been praying for my wife and you sound like her," when she has been earnestly praying to the Lord seeking a husband for herself? All this marriage talk in the first few conversations gave the appearance that we were on the same page. Yet when the relationship became more intense, he told me he was not dating for marriage, he just wanted a woman to call his own. You should have seen my face.

GUARDING YOUR HEART VS. TRUST ISSUES

By now it should be pretty clear that guarding your heart is not at all the same as having unresolved or unacknowledged trust issues with men. Trust issues do not stem from what the Holy Spirit is revealing or what is being revealed by the man's words and actions. Trust issues stem from past experiences and are based entirely on what another man has done that has nothing to do with the present relationship. I talked a lot in Rule #4 Trusting Your Discernment, about trust issues, but as it relates to guarding your heart, here is an easy chart to help pinpoint exactly what you may be experiencing:

Guarding Your Heart	Unresolved Trust Issues
Slowly and gracefully giving more of yourself as you are led by Holy Spirit & Wisdom	Slowly giving more of yourself because you fear he will hurt you
Acknowledging signs, warnings and promptings from your spirit & Holy Spirit	Creating signs and warnings in your mind based solely on a past experience
Mutually opening up to one another as the relationship progresses	Staying completely closed off until the man fully opens up to you
Since you are guarding your heart - you are slow to speak and quick to listen	Since you believe this man is just like other men who have hurt you or someone else close to you - you are slow to speak and quick to listen

There are some fine lines and some situations may seem to fit in a complicated gray area. The two determining factors to pay attention to are your motive and your thought process behind your actions and behaviors. If I ask you why you have chosen to omit certain information about yourself on the first or even fifth date, your response would be telling. If I ask you why you believe a man has shown himself to be untrustworthy, if your response has nothing to do with true spiritual revelations or blatant actions (that have not been misinterpreted) and has everything to do with an ex, your past or what you have witnessed in another relationship, you may have to rethink how you are processing information. You don't want to drive away a good man, but you also don't want to end up like I did with the deacon, mired in self-deception.

Even though there is a fine balancing act, you can rest assured that God is with you and he has your back. He will make it crystal clear whether a man is true or not. He will also make it clear if there are areas within yourself that you need to work on before you start getting to know or dating any man at all.

Rest and trust in the Lord. He is your leader, guide and ultimate protector.

RULE #12:

NEVER REPLACE GOD WITH A MAN

The worst thing a woman can do is serve, worship and love God with her all as a single woman and then once she starts dating and falls in love, place God on the back burner of her life. Many unequally yoked marriages started out this way. The woman was at one time totally devoted to God. She was God fearing and passionate about the Lord yet longing for love. Once love came into her life, slowly but surely her time with God began to dwindle and her new man replaced God on the throne of her heart.

This type of woman tells herself that even though her new man is not where she is spiritually, she will pray for him and enjoy his company. She will continue to focus on God, even as she dates him. She begins to give her heart to him and even though she notices that her prayer and study time has lessened because she is now spending more quality time with her man, she continues to move forward in the relationship. She loves God. And now, she loves her man. Her man is not on the same page as she is spiritually, so he doesn't understand her lifestyle of worship and at times, expects her to choose him over God, without explicitly stating so. They hang out late Saturday night and she is too tired for church, so she and her love go to brunch instead. She normally studies her bible and reads 1-2 books per month to help her grow spiritually, but since she is spending so much time traveling with her new man and mingling with his friends and family, her personal bible study time suffers and her book reading declines.

In the worst-case scenario, the woman would have made a personal vow to God to keep herself until marriage, making a firm decision not to have sex until she is a married woman. Yet, because of the differences in conviction, teaching, understanding as well as submission to the Word God, the couple disagree and eventually, the woman gives in to the man's desires: sex now, not after marriage. He believes there is nothing wrong with sex at this point in their relationship because they are now in love.

As the woman finds herself drifting further and further from God, yet closer to her new man, she decides to continue on this path towards marriage and simply hopes it will all work out in the end and eventually her new man will come around, her prayers will be answered, and sometime in the near future she can get back to worshipping God again. This is a horrible deception.

The reality is that when you sacrifice a piece of yourself

or your spirituality to be with a man, you cannot get it back. The man you marry has fallen in love with the woman you have shown him you are. You are the woman that puts him before God. You are the woman who has stated she had certain convictions that have led to godly lifestyle choices, yet little by little, you have shown this man that his needs come first and/or you are willing to disregard your convictions all together in order to please him or be with him. You must understand that even though you're not saying the words "I am putting my man before God," if your actions reveal pleasing him before or above what you know God desires for you to do, that is in fact what you are doing.

When a woman loses her lifestyle of worshipping God to be with a man, she ends up marrying, she regrets it. I have seen this on many, many occasions, firsthand. The new wife settles into married life with a man who doesn't share her views on God, service, worship or lifestyle and many more conflicts begin to arise because of the lack of spiritual oneness. She hopes to get back to God, but as soon as she begins to pursue a new true relationship with Christ, the husband is upset and possibly non-supportive because she is trying to take time from her new family for the Lord. He never understood her spiritual needs, and the promises she made to God were not significant to him. Now he feels slighted, neglected and possibly unsupportive because he does not agree with the personal changes she is making now. He also will not understand why it's "all of a sudden" so important that she make these changes when they have been coasting along fine all the time they have been together. In his mind, they were coasting along fine, towards the same path. In her mind, she was disappointing God or giving up portions of her relationship with God to be with him but hoping to get back on track once they were married, or once all of her intercessory prayers for him were answered.

Another example is the woman who is zealous about the things of God and serves God passionately with her life. That is, because she is single and waiting to meet a good man. She is only "content" with her singleness because she believes the season will be short lived. She is only on fire for God because she believes God will send her to her husband by the end of that particular year. She is not fully rooted in her love and service for God which will be made apparent as soon as she has a new man-friend. You will not see her at as many church functions, events and services. She may bring her new man-friend to church with her and you will notice her pulling back on her zealous servitude. Indeed, she was only serving God passionately as she awaited a man to come into her life.

The Bible teaches us that we are to love the Lord our God with all of our heart, soul and strength. The word "strength" has been translated as effort and passion in some Bible translations. To love the Lord with all that you are is the ultimate goal and desire from the Father. He wants to be on the throne of your heart, even though he placed the desire for marriage within your heart. You should never love a man with all your heart, soul, effort, and strength and only give crumbs or nothing at all to God.

THE BALANCING ACT

There is balance that is required in making time for a new man and maintaining your relationship with God in a way so as not to neglect either God or your new boo. I taught previously about making physical time for love in your life in Rule #10 Make Room For Love, so I will focus more on the spiritual aspects here.

It is possible to invest time and effort into your relationship while maintaining quality time in prayer simultaneously. There is also nothing wrong with interceding for your new man, but only as you are led, so he is not consuming all your spiritual energy and effort. You don't want to see him as a personal spiritual project or make him your new ministry assignment. You have to continue to focus on the first ministry to which you have been called even while you are dating and building a new relationship. There is certainly nothing wrong with adding your agreement with him about his career and business endeavors, covering him in prayer if he is under the weather, or simply praying that God would continue the good work he has begun in his heart, mind, and spirit. Intercession is never wrong, but as always, you want to examine your motives and maintain balance in service.

You also do not want to become his spiritual covering and leader. He should have a pastor and spiritual mentor to meet his spiritual needs, in addition to his personal relationship with Christ. The difference between praying for him as you are led and being his spiritual leader, is that you pray from a mind and heart of peace with no ulterior motive. If you are praying for him to be a strong man of God because he is currently a man who is far from God and you see him as your husband one day, that is the sole reason you are praying for him and giving him bible scriptures. Or you may see great potential in him and desire to see that potential realized ASAP so that you can get married sooner rather than later. Your motives are selfish and your prayers are marriage driven. On the other hand, when you pray as you are led, there is pure intention and you are encouraging him with prayer, not trying to lead and cover him spiritually.

There is also an emotional balance when the relationship becomes more involved, which is the balance of loving God with your all and falling in love with a man. Keep in mind that even though you will begin to give more of yourself as the relationship progresses towards marriage, you should never give all of yourself to a man that is not yet your husband. Your husband will not replace God on the throne of your heart either. Once the two of you become one, you will both love God with your all together, as one. You will be "one" in spirit, soul and mind after marriage. And as you each love and serve each other and the family, you will be also loving and serving God with your all at the very same time.

You should be able to tell when you are starting to go too far with your intimacy, giving and interactions with your man. There should be a clear difference between what you are giving in the relationship now and what you will give after you become his wife. If the line is so narrow and blurry it's almost non-existent, that means you are giving and doing too much. Think about it like this: you should leave him wanting more and more of you that he can only experience once he not only proposes, but officially makes you his wife.

He should not be fully satisfied with you only as his girlfriend/ fiancée because he knows there are other levels of satisfaction and enjoyment he will receive after you are married. Leaving this space will also ensure that you are not placing him above God at any point in the relationship, even as you are growing closer and falling more and more in love with him.

SPIRITUAL FLOW

One of the reasons I highly recommend getting into a spiritual flow with God now while you are single is because once you are married, you will have less time than you do now. Your life is already full; full of work, business, ministry, service, family, friends, self-care, fitness, education, and personal time with God. You probably could add to this list when you think about other areas of your life that consistently require your time and energy. If you have children already, your time restraints are even more significant. Spiritually speaking, you cannot allow your time with God to slip in any season because your personal time with God is what makes you the strong Christian woman that you are.

Your time with God gives birth to personal revelations which fuels your faith, prophetic words and visions, which is a call to intercession or prophetic ministry, private convictions as you study the Word that when obeyed, leads to spiritual maturity and an abundance of encouragement with infusions of spiritual strength that is given only by Holy Spirit during moments of true worship. Once you are married, not only do you need to make personal time for God, but you now must include providing for the spiritual needs of your family, just like the Proverbs 31 woman. You are not to cover the family spiritually, but you must contribute powerfully to the spiritual fabric of the home.

As a single woman, you pray for yourself and others as you are led. As a wife you pray for yourself, your husband and children, and then others as you are led. Not only do you have to walk in the love of Christ outside of your home, but now you have to operate in God-kind-of-love day in and day out within your home. Your spiritual plate becomes fuller than ever.

If you did not get into a good flow with your relationship with God as a single woman, the spiritual role you have as a wife can be very overwhelming for you.

RULE #13:

TAKE YOUR TIME AND DON'T RUSH

T he beginning of a new relationship is so exciting. You're happy to have the undivided attention of a handsome man of God and it feels amazing to know you are desired and not invisible. This is especially true if any length of time has passed since you have dated someone seriously or been involved with any man.

After the first long, late-night conversation you wonder: is he the one? After the first, second or even sixth amazing date, you wonder: is he the one? You daydream about what life would be like if your worlds were to unite and how your lives would flow happily and perfectly (in your mind) together once you're married. You imagine taking trips together, discussing finances and making investments together, him being an amazing father to your children and the type of bonus mother you would be to his children. You see yourself attending church together, or even serving in the ministry as a couple. Your vision continues as you think through family holiday rotations, hosting your future in-laws or where you would travel for different celebrations throughout the year. You may even consider the type of area you would agree to settle down in, considering what you have learned are his likes and dislikes in a home or geographical location. I could go on, but I will stop there.

Most women have these types of thoughts very early on in a relationship, during the friendship phase, and long before the man is even considering whether you two will enter a committed, serious relationship or not. Matters are worsened if the man appears to be everything you have on your list or more. But here's the thing. You won't know if he is truly the man on your list until some time has passed and you have allowed God to reveal and confirm the type of man he truly is, whether he is called to be your future husband or whether he is a counterfeit from the devil.

You must slow down your thoughts, daydreams and visions long enough to get to know the man thoroughly. This may seem impossible in the midst of blessed excitement but here are some things you can do to help you to slow down.

Try not to read into his words and actions, making them bigger and more significant than they are. You may know what I mean here. He invites you to church one day and you think he is making a public display of his affection, telling the world he is off the market and settling down; when in reality, he was only inviting you to church much like he would any other new friend. Or let's say one day he cooks and invites you over. You think he is cooking to show affection and give you insight on what he would be like as a husband; when in reality he likes to cook and cooks for anyone, anytime. In his mind, he is getting to know you, not making a display of future husband-hood.

Pace yourself. Don't allow the new friendship to consume all your time and energy. This is almost self-explanatory, especially if you lead a full life. Pace yourself in the beginning so that you are not giving too much time and sacrificing all that has become important to you, even as you continue to get to know him and allow the relationship room to bloom.

Get to know him as a man, son of God, and citizen first. Before you try to determine whether he would be a good husband and before you start to daydream about raising a family, take enough time to learn who he is as a person first. Lots of amazing chemistry can be tricky and misleading, but a lack of chemistry is also notable and should help you ease into a deeper relationship with him.

Here are two real life examples of occasions when I made the mistake of moving too fast in relationships and ended up with hurt feelings due to misunderstandings that were not entirely the man's fault.

A MAN IN TRANSITION

In one case, during my twenties, I was in a relationship with a man who was still getting back on his feet after a major, long-term relationship with his live-in fiancée ended. She broke up with him, but since she had children, he moved out of their home and back with his mother. He also was in school getting certified as an X-ray technician and held a part time job in the meantime with very limited hours. Any man who is fresh out of a long-term, committed relationship or in between jobs is not thinking about marriage. He is thinking about himself, the past and figuring out exactly what he is going to do with his future. I entered into a relationship with him, only thinking about my own desires and where I was in life. I was successful in my career, finished with my professional degree, was graduating from bible school and was living a single, celibate, and exciting life serving in ministry at a high capacity.

We had amazing chemistry and he was someone I had known for a number of years. It was easy for me to imagine our future lives together and what it would be like if I became a bonus mom to his children. I saw myself covering his children in prayer and being a good godly example for his daughter (her mother had passed away and he had full custody of her). I imagined him being an amazing protector and provider. I always felt safe with him and we discussed financial management ideas together. I allowed my thoughts, and therefore my actions, to accelerate well beyond the place where he was concerning our relationship.

But as things progressed, it became painfully obvious that I was living in a dream world and rushing progress. We had many disagreements about spiritual matters and lifestyle choices. This was the season I learned there was a sharp disparity in my belief system (I am a non-denominational Christian woman) and the traditional Baptist belief system. Although we were both Christians, we were, in fact, not equally yoked. He also had underlying temper, self-control, and lust issues I wasn't aware of until time went on. Once we parted ways, I felt incredibly foolish for even thinking that he was the husband God had for me and believing that my prayers had been answered.

A FALSE POSITIVE RELATIONSHIP

On another occasion, because of little coincidences early in the friendship, I just "knew" God was in the midst. We were introduced by a family member, he lived on Foxworth Road, he was the perfect height, had the right finances and career type, and went to church and sought to go higher in God on his own. This relationship was so peaceful and easygoing, it took a few months before more and more layers were pulled back and it became evident that he was not the husband God had in mind for me. He was not mature spiritually at all, even though he was a mature man (in age and worldly wisdom). He had weak areas that the Lord himself revealed through discernment and these were areas he was not willing to work on or even acknowledge as being an issue. He was set in his ways. We also did not agree on children, how many to have or how to raise them.

What I learned in that relationship was #1: not to confuse maturity that comes with age with spiritual maturity. It can be hard to decipher between the two, which is why discernment is key. Additionally, discussing spiritual topics such as gifts of the Spirit, prayer tongues, hearing God's voice and serving ministry provide a clear picture of where a man is located spiritually speaking. The second thing I learned was a powerful lesson about reading too much into a man's intention just because he is excited about me. A man can be very interested in you, and like you a lot. He has fun with you, you are fine in his eyes, he likes talking to you and sharing dreams and goals with you. He may even go out of his way for you and make sacrifices to make you happy. But, all these things are normal relationship behavior, it doesn't mean he intends to propose anytime soon.

Oh, how I fooled myself in this season! After several months of this easygoing relationship, I just "knew" he was going to propose to me. I was even going to overlook his lack of spiritual maturity and be satisfied with his natural maturity (he was almost a decade older), but that would have been a horrible choice. Once I realized he had no intention of proposing anytime soon and that he still needed quite a bit more time to decide if I was wife material for him, I started to notice much more clearly the lack of spiritual unity. We were not on the same page spiritually and although he was a mature man, he was a spiritual baby. It was not possible for him to cover me spiritually because he was so new to the faith. Although my daydreams were filled with raising a God-fearing family, it became apparent that he could in no way lead a family spiritually because of his lack of conviction, knowledge, and personal revelations. Our relationship even ended in a very immature manner with me unable to reach him and therefore having to break up with him on a voicemail and then never hearing from him again.

In both of these relationships, I broke all three of the cardinal rules stated earlier. I read way too much into their actions towards me, I didn't pace myself and rushed ahead, and I started seeing them as a husband, instead of learning the fullness of who they were just as men, friends, sons of God and citizens. Both relationships ended with hurt feelings on both sides, which may have been avoided if I had taken my time and stopped rushing, built a blessed friendship first and then slowly entered into a deeper relationship at a mutual pace.

RULE #14:

ACKNOWLEDGE AND BREAK
GENERATIONAL CURSES

A generational curse is a propensity towards a certain type of sin, behavior or bondage that is not of God. Plainly stated it's an ungodly behavior or thought process that comes almost naturally and can be found throughout prior generations of your bloodline. These curses are spiritual in nature and not brought on by any external source. If you were to look throughout the family, including immediate, extended and the 3rd and 4th generations prior, you will notice a similar or the same ungodly lifestyle, struggle, or bondage. Examples include addictions, poverty, mental health issues, sexual sins including homosexuality, anxiety, rebellion and even having multiple children with multiple men outside of wedlock. I have witnessed abuse of all types manifest throughout generations as well as similar or the same insecurities.

It's important to acknowledge any generational curses in your own bloodline so that you are keenly aware of your weak areas and propensities to sin or disobey God. When you are mindful of these things, you can steer clear of any relationship or person who would feed your weaknesses, enabling poor choices, bad behavior and disastrous consequences that would detour or even cancel God's plan for your life. If you were to ignore or disregard generational curses, you will easily fall into Satan's plans and traps.

The good news is that Jesus has already redeemed us from generational curses and provided the opportunity to begin living in generational blessings on the day of our salvation. When we are born again, our old nature is abolished and so goes the propensity to sin. However, the enemy is still going to attempt to ensnare us in those same bloodline curses using familiar tactics. He wants it to appear as if we have not been freed from generational curses and as if the struggle for freedom is too difficult to maintain.

Here's a real life example of a generational curse that runs in my bloodline which I have broken, by the grace and power of God: addiction. Although I did not know anything about my great grandparents, I can trace the curse back at least three generations. When I started smoking small, flavored cigars at 16 years of age, I

SCAN ME

Watch the video about breaking the spirit of delay brought on by generational curses

didn't know anything about what a generational curse was. I could not explain why when I hung out and partied with my friends, I always went overboard with drinking alcohol and smoking (weed and nicotine). I wanted to drink and smoke all the time, whereas my friends could just hang out and have fun without the extra activities. I would only want to hang out with men that could give us access to these things and I would initiate the process of getting high while we were just hanging out with these men, even if they had no intentions of doing those things with us. I used to wonder why my friends didn't enjoy it as much as I did. Sure, they would participate, but they would not indulge at the level I did and they could go without it. I wanted to drink and smoke every time we hung out and I wanted to get as high as possible for as long as possible.

No one around me participated in such activities. No one in my household drank liquor or smoked anything. My friends' parents did not drink or smoke anything. The desire and craving came swiftly after one taste, a moment in time I cannot even remember. All I remember is that I couldn't get enough. I believe it was the protection of God that only allowed me access to alcohol and weed. If I had the opportunity to partake of a stronger substance, God only knows where my life would have ended up. However, others in my bloodline were not as lucky. Alcohol, illicit drug use and nicotine addiction are very real chains of bondage still evident in the lives of certain family members of my own generation and the one just before us.

3 STEPS TO BREAKING GENERATIONAL CURSES

There are three things that are needed to break generational curses successfully and permanently:

1. Salvation through the saving grace of Christ Jesus. You must receive Jesus Christ as your personal Lord and savior. Once your spirit is born-again, the old nature is no more and you receive the new nature of Christ. This means, you are now abiding under a generational blessing through your new spiritual inheritance, old things have passed away, and all things have become new. Here is a simple prayer you can pray in accordance with Romans: 10:9-10 to receive salvation in Christ Jesus:

   Heavenly Father, thank you for loving me and calling me into your beautiful kingdom. I confess with my mouth and believe in my heart that Jesus is Lord, that he died for my sins and rose on the third day with all power in his hands, so that I might be saved. Today I receive my salvation and a new, born-again spirit in you. I thank you that every generational curse is broken, and I now live in the generational blessing of Christ Jesus. In Jesus' name, Amen!

2. Pray and speak out loud that the generational curses over your life (and your children's lives) have been broken. Apply the blood of Jesus over those generational bloodline curses you have identified. Whenever you feel attacked in your mind or spirit, confess your freedom. If you feel overwhelmed by the attacks, seek mature believers who can agree with you in prayer. Remember that you have already been delivered from generational curses on the day of your salvation. These verbal declarations and prayers are to help you maintain your

freedom and not fall back into old habits. These prayers and confessions will also help you to access wisdom from God about how you can stay free.

3. This leads me into the third point of breaking generational curses. Create a lifestyle that supports and encourages your freedom and makes it difficult for the enemy to ensnare you in those ungodly habits and behaviors. This is a huge part of your freedom and is often overlooked or disregarded. Using myself as an example, if I want to maintain freedom from addiction, I cannot date or marry a man who drinks and smokes, even if it's only recreationally. I cannot be with a man who parties and enjoys the company of others who drink and smoke. Even if those friends are only drinking wine with dinner and smoking hookah for fun, it would not be wise for me to be with a man in that environment if I want to maintain my freedom from all generational curses that I have broken through salvation, prayer and personal lifestyle choices.

When you are dating a man and you are right at the point of deciding whether you want to be in a committed relationship exclusively or not, you must also start looking for clues that reveal generational curses that are evident or even better, clues of the generational blessing by way of Jesus Christ. To make it simple, if you look at the life and lifestyle maintained by your new man and compare it to the life that his parents and grandparents lived, what are the key differences? Now on one hand, let's say he comes from an amazing family of God-fearing people who love God and live blessed and fruitful lives. His family is not perfect by any means, but they have family traditions that you would want to marry into and pass down to your children.

On the other hand, if his family has signs of brokenness, struggle, poor decisions, sickness and health challenges, poverty, rebellion or even idol worship, you have to take this into strong consideration. Even though those things are still evident in his bloodline, has he himself broken free from all generational curses? Has he begun to live his life in alignment with the generational blessing or does he still struggle to break free and shift?

It's always okay to pray and intercede for him as you are led but be careful not to take on too much spiritual responsibility for his personal breakthrough. When you care for him, you want the best for him and you may begin to see yourself as a vital addition to his life for the purpose of helping him reach his full potential in multiple ways. But I caution you: if he is not actively working to break any remnants of blatant generational curses on his own, your presence and persistence will become more and more counterproductive.

There is a level of spiritual maturity that is obtained as you break free from any and all generational curses. Like all spiritual growth, transformation of one's spirit, mind and heart is a work by and through the Holy Spirit. The initiation of great change in your man's life must be birthed from within his spirit as he responds to the Holy Spirit...not a love interest. Again, I am not saying that you shouldn't support or encourage him, just remember that the work must begin with his own personal decision and choices followed by significant lifestyle changes. Trying to force feed spiritual knowledge and breakthrough, even through love, will not work.

While we are all a work in progress and none of us are perfect, you want to make sure that you are both not struggling with the same weak areas. You don't want to enable one another in sin, but the goal is to be better together. Remember your future marriage is all about ministry, both within the family and without. So whether you are currently in a season of waiting for your husband to find you, or on the brink of committing to a serious relationship, start acknowledging and addressing your own generational blessings and curses in preparation for the manifestation of the marriage you are praying for.

RULE #15:

HAVE THE HARD CONVERSATIONS SOONER, RATHER THAN LATER

You already know how important communication is in relationships. When major issues are unacknowledged or unaddressed, a relationship crumbles. When hard conversations are avoided during the onset of a relationship or as it deepens, those hidden concerns eventually surface, potentially with shocking resolve. What I am not suggesting is that you bring up conversations appropriate for the courtship phase when you're still building a new friendship. Yet, especially for mature women, there are conversations you must have earlier than you did before to ensure you are compatible and share similar goals and values for the foreseeable future.

Many women avoid certain topics of conversation so as not to "scare away" a potential life partner. What I have learned after many years of study and real-life experience is that when you are getting to know a mature man of God, you can't scare him away by inquiring about his values, desires, and goals. Of course you must always use wisdom in approaching sensitive topics and properly gauge the pace of your relationship to make sure you're not moving too fast with your emotions. But when God brings you together with the man he has ordained for you to build a future with and marry, you will both be on the same page, even early on. You may even find that he brings up certain topics of conversation, even those hard conversations, before you do, because he is seriously dating for marriage.

One thing is for sure: you want to have these hard conversations before you fully give away your heart and start to fall in love with the man. It's devastating when you find yourself fully committed and invested in a relationship, only to learn that the conversations you avoided so as not to scare him off, or face what you believe will be an unpleasant turn of events, begin to shed light on your incompatibility. You both have deal breakers. Some are clearly evident on the surface. Others only come out through clear and concise communication.

Hard conversation topics to consider:

- Do you both want children or more children if you already have any? How many?
- Are you both celibate? Do you share a revelation on keeping your body for marriage in obedience to God, or is it only about keeping the other person?
- What do you each believe about what exactly defines abuse or heated disagreements?
- What are the father's and mother's roles when it comes to raising children and teaching them the ways of God?
- Are you on the same page about earning, investing, saving, distributing, and spending money? What about tithing, sowing, and reaping?
- What do you believe about how to worship and serve the Lord? How do you both worship God in your lifestyle choices and daily living?
- What do you believe about legacy, inheritance, and generational wealth?
- Is there anything in either of your pasts that is questionable, illegal or should be disclosed (and discussed/explained) rather than discovered accidentally?
- What do you each believe about caring and providing for your parents/family once they are elderly?

These are some examples of hard questions which of course will vary based on the specific man and how your relationship is evolving. These questions go in both directions as well. Some women tend to share too much too soon, while others are so closed off, the man suffers from a lack of emotional intimacy. In between these two extremes is fine balance and wisdom to confirm or reveal matters that either need to be worked through and further discussed or incompatibility altogether.

Now once you have had the hard conversation, how to tell whether you should pump the brakes, call it quits or keep moving forward is a personal (and spiritual) decision. No one can or should make this decision for you and you should never feel pressured to stay in a situation where there are extreme compromises. When God said he would give you the desires of your heart in Psalm 37:4, he meant exactly that. Compromising that leads to peace and happiness is one thing but compromising that would ultimately lead you to resentment and regret is not worth it in the long run. You don't want to end up married and later wonder if God possibly had a better option for you if you waited a bit longer.

Also keep in mind, a mature man of God will understand that you are discussing these topics because they are important to your future together, not because you are trying to push him away or embarrass him in any way. The goal is never to hold anything against anyone, but to locate exactly where the person is today regarding their lifestyle, beliefs, and actions.

Here's my real-life example. I was in a relationship with a mature man of God and had to probe in one conversation to understand how he ended up with three children by two different women (one was his ex-wife) and the two youngest children were the same age. Long story short, he was married, wanted to leave the marriage (but never officially divorced or separated) so he physically left the home, got together with a new woman who became pregnant, then returned home to work things out with his wife the same year. In other words, he had a love child, although he didn't consider himself cheating because he "left."

When I probed simply to understand the history of this 14-year prior situation, he was very defensive. I explained to him that I wasn't trying to label him or hold anything against him, but I could learn more about his mindset and belief system concerning marriage, divorce and cheating as he explained what happened. I told him that my concern was about both what he was thinking back then and what he thinks today or if he still held the same beliefs and behaviors.

He remained defensive for the entire conversation. I believe he really had made peace about his choices, or he secretly still felt that what he did was alright. I ended the conversation to avoid an unnecessary conflict, but his response definitely gave me pause. If he came clean and admitted his mistakes on his own, without me having to do a lot of probing (as he beat around the bush) and if he had not been so defensive but rather explained the situation and life lessons learned, the conversation would have gone more smoothly and there would have been no need to virtually side eye him (we had this talk over the phone).

Tips for Hard Conversations

- Use lots of wisdom in your approach, tone, and timing.
- Ask probing questions, don't assume anything.
- Don't avoid topics based on bad or fear-based advice.
- If you have a Spirit-filled man of God in your life, get his personal advice on how to approach the conversation.

I want to reiterate an earlier point and that is, you don't have to worry that these hard conversations will scare off the right man for you. They will locate the wrong man quickly. But the right man, a mature man, doesn't mind discussing topics that are important to you, as they should be important to him as well. They might not be on the same level of importance, or perhaps he doesn't have a firm stance and is flexible concerning the area of discussion, but one thing is for sure, your concerns will not scare or intimidate him.

I heard a man of God speak about a similar topic a few years ago. He stated how his wife is very intellectual, intense, motivated and driven and those are the things that separated her from other women and attracted him to her more than anything. He said that he would never say while dating that his wife was "too much" for him because that statement was a good thing. He wanted a woman to keep him on his toes and challenge him in diverse ways. They have been married for over 14 years and he still frequently declares how he is a better man because of his wife being a partner in his life.

Lastly, the older you get while single and dating, the more important it is to have the hard conversations earlier on in a budding relationship. You don't want to get deep into a relationship and fall in love, only to find out that you have your heart set on having two children and he does not want children at all. Or you find out that although he wants to be in a committed relationship with you, his divorce taught him that he never wants to get married again. Or you find that you are on two totally different pages concerning earning, saving, investing, and spending money. What if he cheats on his taxes and you are a woman of integrity? What if you believe in tithing and sowing in the kingdom of God and he believes pastors only scam Christians out of money? What if his past is checkered? True, everyone can repent and build a new life, but how far removed is he from his old life? You may be in for much more than you bargained for if you don't discuss these things soon.

RULE #16:

NO MORE EXCUSES

D on't make excuses for red-flag issues or throw your deal breakers in the trash can. How many times have you been in a relationship, noticed red flags early on but chose to ignore them? Or maybe you had your relationship deal-breakers that turned into ne-gotiables and later were totally removed in order to keep a man or relationship. These types of concessions never work out well. Many women live in regret and now have to sever soul ties, heal from heartbreak and devastation, or deal with life-long consequences of those decisions.

You may be the young woman who has not yet had a real relationship, so consider this section a strong warning not to repeat the mistakes of your older sisters in Christ. Here are common excuses women have made for men that ended up blowing up in their face as the relationship progressed and ultimately crumbled:

- He is not where you need him to be spiritually (he is not able to teach, lead or cover you in the things of God at all) but you are very understanding and decide to be patient, pray, and share your revelations with him.

- He is not physically attractive, but you convince yourself that maybe God is sending you someone "different" than what you have been praying for, because it is what's best for you. (As if God's best for you is someone you don't think is a little bit handsome or attractive).

- He is not financially where you would need him to be to build a family, but you decide that since you make good money, you will support him, pray for him and patiently wait on his potential to manifest.

- He struggles with controlling his temper, mood swings, alcohol, or drug consumption or even his faithfulness (he has cheated before) but you decide to stay and pray for him, patiently waiting on God to help him get a breakthrough and be transformed into the man you know he can be.

- He is a very nice and good man, but his personality is not fun, exciting or stimulating for you. You find yourself feeling bored most of the time and wondering if this relationship is as good as it will get, because you have been single for so long. You believe your life with him would be fine, but it wouldn't be the fun love affair you have always dreamed of.

- He is not good with his children or very interested in your children, but he adores you. Although you would like him to engage more with your children and be more mindful of their needs, you are so happy to have a man who is focused on you, you decide to compromise in this area. After all, your children already have a father and this will be your husband.

- He is not celibate and has no conviction against having sex prior to marriage, but you decide to stay and try your best not to sleep with him. You find yourself participating in all kinds of questionable sexual activities with him that bring you much guilt and conviction or even worse, you end up sleeping with him, breaking your personal promise of celibacy and holiness to God.

These situations are all red-flags indicating that the re-lationship will not produce the loving, strong, God-glorifying marriage you desire, but you make excuse after excuse, praying and hoping that things will change. The problem is that you should never enter a relationship expecting such changes to manifest in order for you to be fully happy and satisfied. These types of concessions should give you pause and make you strongly reconsider whether God is involved in the relationship at all. No relationship is perfect, yet you should never have to make excuses for a man in order to be with him.

Another good way to identify a red flag that should not be ignored, is when there are aspects of the relationship or the man's lifestyle that you keep hidden from those who are close to you. You are either embarrassed, ashamed, or feeling guilty about your decision, so you choose to keep secrets or situations between the two of you. This is a very clear and obvious sign that your relationship will not bring you peace (a secret life is not peaceful) or be able to minister to souls the way God designed it to.

Let's consider again Ephesians chapter 5: God's plan and purpose for marriage. When you find yourself making excuses for, overlooking, or managing red-flags and trying to patiently pray through major issues, your marriage will not reflect how much God loves his church. Your relationship pre-marriage is not a reflection of Christ's love for his people or how a man is supposed to wash his wife with the water of the Word and make her holy. If those things are not taking place while you are dating and courting, they will not magically begin to take place after you're married.

Here's my real-life example and very transparent moment. When I entered into a relationship with my male best friend of 17 years, I knew he was not the type of man I would want to marry as-is. There was a reason we were only friends for those 17 years, and there were clear signs that he could not be the man I was praying for and had been in faith for. Yet, because I had been single and celibate for 6 years straight, I chose to disregard my deal-breakers and bypass those glaring red stop signs, plunging straight into a relationship. I did this because of who he was in my life. He was at best friend status and that made him special.

Spiritually speaking, he claimed to believe in Jesus Christ as Lord and savior, yet came from a cultural-generational false god worshipping heritage which he still believed and heavily participated in. He was not a man that was close to God. He had no prayer life, didn't study the Bible, and only went to church when I asked on rare occasions. Yet, I believe I could pray for the spiritual stuff since we had such great chemistry.

Financially, he was nowhere near where he would need to be in order to provide for a family (whether with me or anyone else for that matter), but again I chose to look past it and encouraged his potential. I made the excuse for him that perhaps all he needed was me as his good woman by his side to help him accomplish more as a businessman. I believed my influence was missing from his life and with my support and prayers he could realize all the amazing business goals and dreams he always spoke of.

Mentally and emotionally, he had a strong soul tie with his children's mom and he was an abusive narcissist. Of course, in the beginning, I didn't know or believe any of these things as I made excuses for his behavior and tried to be patient, understanding, and ever so prayerful when I noticed patterns of dishonest communication and hurtful emotional outbursts.

The constant excuses, hiding the true nature of our problems, and continuous supplications to God are how I ended up breaking my six-year celibacy walk and becoming pregnant. I learned a hard lesson in that season. Making excuses for a man, trying to pray him through his issues, and staying even when the relationship begins to hurt is not in the will of God for any of his daughters. We must learn to accept a man at face value and believe that whomever he presents himself to us as is who is really is. Our prayers cannot change a man. Our belief in him will not help him reach his potential. Our faith will not cause him to become strong in the Lord. All of these changes have to start from within his own mind, soul, and spirit. He must have his own will and be working actively on transforming with and for God on his own.

When the excuses you make for a man start to pile up to the point that you are keeping parts of the relationship a secret, that is a sign. When God brings you together with a true man of God, you will be able to brag about him and boast in the Lord. Your relationship will be a testimony of God's goodness, not a situation that leaves you confused about whether God is in the midst or not.

When you sow to the flesh, you reap of the flesh corruption (Galatians 6:8). When you ignore red flags, those chickens will come home to roost. Those concessions you made will come back to bite you in the butt. Get my point? It's not worth it. It's much better to walk away when you see red-flags and continue to trust God for his best, a truly blessed relationship that is red-flag-free and requires no excuses.

RULE #17:

CONFIRM IF HE IS THE ONE

After working your way through all the prior Smart Dating Rules, you should have more than enough food for thought, biblical references, and real-life examples to help you identify what to look for in a God-ordained relationship. An over-simplified summary of what to look for is:

♡ His spiritual maturity. Can he teach, pray for, and lead your family spiritually?

♡ Your compatibility with each other. In every area of your lives, are you physically, mentally, and emotionally compatible?

♡ Your parenting needs and style. Do you have the same goals regarding having and raising children?

♡ His financial situation and beliefs. Can he provide for your family and are you on the same page concerning how you earn, save, spend, invest and sow your money?

♡ If and how your relationship glorifies God. Is your union a testimony of God's goodness and will it help others grow closer to God if they follow the example your relationship presents?

Remember that in accordance with Ephesians Chapter 5, God's overall purpose for marriage is to reflect how much Christ loves the church. Christ's love for us is not based on mere emotion. His love is evident in the self-sacrifice during his crucifixion in addition to the patience, endurance and kindness continually shown to us, his children, on a daily basis. Your relationship will not be perfect by any means, but the love between you should be evident and move beyond the mere feelings of emotional and personal satisfaction.

SPIRITUAL CONFIRMATION

Spiritual confirmation will come directly from the Spirit of God but can come in diverse forms. Likened to any other area of your life in which you receive spiritual confirmation, God can and will speak through any of the following methods:

- Through the written Word, as you study the Bible
- Through the spoken word, a prophetic word spoken to you via the still small voice of God
- Through a dream or vision
- Through a word of prophecy from a person ministering to you under the anointing of the Holy Spirit
- Through the promptings of the Holy Spirit within your born-again spirit, such as discernment, peace, and rest

You want to make sure that you don't rely on only one form of spiritual confirmation. This will prevent you from being deceived by the devil or misled by your emotions or a false word of prophecy.

Above all, keep in mind that God will absolutely speak to you in a manner that you can understand exactly what he wants you to do. God is not the author of confusion and he loves you so very much. Who you give you heart to, marry and have children with is a huge, life altering decision. God does not take your decision lightly. He wants to be involved and clearly order your footsteps. As a matter of fact, I am convinced that God wants to make your path so clear that he will make his intentions known without you even having to ask for confirmation. He is intimately involved with you and absolutely concerned for you (and your current/future children's) wellbeing.

NATURAL CONFIRMATION

I was in a marriage meeting one time and the pastor would ask engaged couples to stand so he could ask them a few questions about their relationship. He would then turn to the woman and ask her, "Is this man the BEST that you can do?" The audience would gasp and get quiet, and the man would nervously look at the pastor and glance at his betrothed.

Obviously in front of an entire congregation her answer would be yes. But that question would give her and every other woman in a serious relationship some food for thought in the days following. Is the man you are considering marrying the very best that you can do? Is he the best that GOD can do? Or have you settled? Are you tired of waiting and just going to marry him because he is "good enough"? Do you believe that God's best could possibly still be out there? Or does the relationship blow your mind in such a powerful way that it is truly the embodiment of Ephesians 3:20?

Natural confirmation is going to come forth in the diverse natural arenas of your life. Your parents, friends, family, therapist, counselor, and other couples may serve as sources of confirmation. The flow of your relationship and the impact that your relationship makes on others, the community, the church family and even your immediate family is also important to examine and acknowledge.

While every person's family may not be filled with the Holy Spirit and they may even have underlying agendas or issues, for the most part you can use both of your families as voices of confirmation. What your parents say of him and how his parents speak of you both is important to consider because your parents know you better than anyone. They literally have been a part of your life longer than any other person. If you (or your significant other) were raised by someone other than your parents, whoever those persons are that serve as your parental figures still will have very valid opinions. Your friends will want the best for you and can be a very eye- opening mirror, describing exactly what they see happening as you grow closer to the man, both the good and the bad.

Additionally, the forward progression of the relationship is one of the biggest ways to get natural confirmation. If your relationship is stagnant and not moving forward on a path towards marriage, that's a sign. I'm not saying that you should discuss your marriage plans during the friendship phase obviously, but at some point, you must make sure that you both are on the same page moving from friends to committed to courting to engaged and eventually to marriage. Good signs include the man making future plans with you and his genuine interest in your family. When he wants to have a relationship with not only you but those who are close to you, that's a great sign. When he begins to speak casually about how he sees himself in your world in the future, that is the best sign of all. He is subtly letting you know that he sees himself in your life for the long haul.

Just like the spiritual areas of confirmation, you want to look for multiple other ways that confirmation will come forth. You can't listen to only one person's opinion, and you also cannot rely solely on what your man is saying and doing.

Even though this section is about natural forms of confirmation, I believe that God is still in the midst of these options. The Lord may lead your therapist or cousin to reveal something about your relationship that you cannot see because you are so close to it. The Lord may cause your man to slip up and reveal his heart, if he is not truly in it for the long haul, or if he has ulterior motives. The Lord can also use as a vessel any person who is or is not privy to the inner workings of your relationship to give a clear reflection of what your relationship is communicating with the world.

It's highly important to make sure that you receive external confirmation, both spiritual and natural before you marry the wrong person. You cannot be led by your emotions alone or even what you perceive to be right or wrong. There are safeguards built into our lives as Christian women that some of you aren't even aware of until God uses them to provide a warning or the final assurance you need to move forward.

Rest assured, God will give you the confirmation you need to move forward into a blessed future with the particular man in question or he will let you know that is not his will and in fact he has better in store for you. You can trust that God knows how to speak to you. He knows how to get a clear message to you. It's up to you to listen and recognize what God is saying and move forward accordingly.

I have been contacted on numerous occasions by women who know that they have married the wrong man. I have worked with and coached many divorced women as well. Every time these women had clear signs against moving forward but ignored those signs because their desire to be married was stronger than their desire to continue to wait on God's very best. As a matter of fact, I have yet to meet a woman that believes the reverse: that God was giving her confirmation that the man was in fact her God-ordained husband, but she chose to follow the wrong signs and decided not to marry him. Most times, when you desire marriage very badly, you may decide to overlook promptings of the Lord or clear communication from those who care for you just to get married.

Here is an easy list of various ways to receive natural confirmation based on each area previously discussed:

♥ Family, friends, and close acquaintances
♥ Your church family, leaders and ministers
♥ Your significant other's friends, family, and close acquaintances
♥ Therapist, counselor, coach or other professional
♥ The natural progression of the relationship you experience
♥ The outwardly spoken plans for your future lives combining as discussed with each other

I will close with the amazing bible love story of how Isaac and Rebekah were brought together by God and the various ways Abraham's servant received confirmation that she was the woman that was to become his wife. You can find the entire biblical account in Genesis Chapter 24.

The story begins with Abraham sending his closest servant to go and find Isaac's wife and bring her back to their land so they could marry and raise a family. There are so many gems in this story, but I will focus only on how exactly the servant received multiple forms of confirmation throughout the entire process.

First, the servant had clear instructions from God about where to find this woman. This was important because her geographic location and her heritage determined what God she served. It was important she was a woman found among the pagan worshippers of that time. Next, the servant was assured that if he was not sure about his selection, he should not fear because an angel of the Lord would go before him amid the situation. The servant was prayerful throughout the entire process, seeking confirmation by looking for certain signs that she was the one. Every little thing that he asked God to give him as confirmation took place. Even when it was time for the woman to make a choice (which would be the final sign of knowing if anyone desires to marry another person) she could have stayed home for another 10 days or left right away to enter into her future life. She chose to move forward and not to stay home. Who knows? If she had asked to stay another 10 days, the servant may have seen that as a sign that he chose wrongly and he needed to find another woman willing to follow the path God laid before her, immediately.

Many fine details about that story differ drastically from modern day culture, not to mention you are a woman seeking confirmation about giving your heart to a man and not a man finding a wife (which are different processes entirely). But you can take key clues from the story of how God not only provides confirmation but desires to be fully involved in every aspect of the relationship and courtship process.

Following a similar process, get instructions for exactly how to go about meeting, dating, and courting utilizing the Word of God (one of the main goals of this book). Following God's instructions will keep you safe and on the right path. Next, stay prayerful throughout the entire relationship. Never think you know more than God or that you don't need God's guidance. In this story we see that God uses angels to lead us. But he also can lead you by your inward witness, the still small voice of God, dreams and visions as well as providing external signs that you are on the right path, or that you need to end the relationship immediately.

Notice that when the servant asked for signs, they had everything to do with the character or the type of woman she was, as well as her own desire and willingness to leave her family and start a new life. Most of us would say, "Yes, I'm ready to go get married!" But remember, when you are courting a man, you need to pay attention to his desire to truly settle down and start a new family with you. You also want to allow God to reveal his character and not make excuses or think you can pray for him to change once you're married. What you see is what you get and it's never a good idea to marry "potential." Notice, the servant didn't ask the Lord to lead him to any beautiful woman and then he would take her home and train her how to be giving and selfless later. She needed to embody those qualities upon their initial encounter.

Take the example and cues given in this bible love story to help you in understanding how God is involved with confirming whether a person is the one or not. Read through the story at least three times, prayerfully, and allow the Holy

Spirit to speak to your heart about your relationship.

It's not hard to tell whether a man is the one sent from God for you to marry or not. The issue only comes when God is clearly saying no, but your emotions are overpowering inner spiritual wisdom or others around you are pressuring you to say yes. Take this question and seriously think about what a truthful answer would be. Is he really the best that you can do?

PART 2:

DATING IN THE MODERN WORLD: HOT TOPICS

RULES FOR LONG DISTANCE DATING

RULE #1:

REMOVE THE DISTANCE AS MUCH AS POSSIBLE

Y ou may be a few hours away by car or a few hundred miles away by plane, but it is possible to have a fun and blessed relationship, even at a long distance. I am often asked about long-distance dating, which is becoming more and more popular in this generation. We connect with people globally almost daily through diverse communication networks and digital technology. It's beautiful how we can connect and meet new people we would never have had the opportunity to engage with only 20 years ago. With these opportunities to meet new love interests comes the availability of removing distance through technology, in addition to physically coming together.

Moving beyond texting and into live phone conversations is highly important, even if you live around the corner from each other. But now you have many free options of video calling which is the best way to communicate until you can come together face to face again.

Speaking of coming together, it's also highly important that you both make a genuine effort to meet as often as your relationship requires to remain healthy. Each of us have different lifestyles and relationship needs and it's important to make sure you have similarities in these areas to maintain balance and peace. Even though you are separated by a long distance, you should both put effort into shortening the distance through visits and creative use of technology as much as it takes to keep the other person reasonably happy. Remember, you will only be long distance for a season.

RULE #2:

POSITIVE PROGRESSION DOES MATTER

Even though you're long distance, the relationship should still progress in a positive direction, growing and flourishing over the course of time. You should still experience the same steady and blessed pace of a local relationship, making realistic concessions due to geographical challenges.

You should still visit each other's homes so you can see exactly how the other person lives and see if you can imagine yourself fully in his world and vice versa. You should still meet each other's friends and families in person.

When it comes to your celibacy journey, I used to think that it was easier for long distance relationships to keep their bodies for the Lord until marriage. But that is not necessarily true. Think about it, you talk often, you imagine yourself meeting and being together all day and night, especially as feelings begin to grow and you start to miss him more and more. When you are in each other's presence you will have many lingering moments of emotion and desire. For this reason, it is even more important to maintain strict boundaries and consider discussing your weaknesses so as to avoid falling into temptation.

Remember that even though you may be dating or in a committed relationship long distance, your relationship should never be stagnant or stuck in place. Positive forward progression is important in any relationship, no matter the distance.

RULE #3:

BRIDGE THE GAP - PERMANENTLY

W e discussed having hard conversations in the previous chapter, and when you're in a long-distance relationship, one of those conversations will include how you will bridge the gap, removing the geographical distance permanently. While you don't want to rush in your relationship, you still want to take time to get to know the man of God and ensure your compatibility. Yet, at the right time you should both be thinking about and considering how exactly you will come together in the long term. After all, you are both dating for the purpose of marriage, right?

Depending on what season of life you are each in when the Lord brings you together, you may or may not have roots planted in a certain area. One person may be heavily in-volved in their community, local church, company, and organizations as well as hold strong family obligations. The other may be more flexible in career and personal commitments or may simply desire a change of pace and fresh start in a new location. Even if you both have deep roots, the Holy Spirit will help you determine who should make the move. You could also decide to both move and meet each other in a new location, exploring a new city and a new, blessed relationship of togetherness. Then once you're married, you will buy a home together and raise children together in this new special place.

I used to think that women were always the ones to make the sacrifice of changing locations and had to follow the man where he was rooted or desired to live. This incorrect belief was based solely on my limited exposure. It is true that I know of more women who live in a city or state, not because they really love the area, but because their husbands did or they had a really good job that was non-transferable. Over the years I have encountered more and more women who were married to men who didn't mind making the trek to wherever she was located in the world and planting new roots. The key is finding a location that works for you both. You both need lucrative careers, the ability to continue building strong family relationships, a church home that you both enjoy, and a living environment where you both experience peace and joy.

If you find yourself in a situation in which you both refuse to budge and relocate for the sake of the relationship, that is a clear sign that he is not the one for you. When it's a God-ordained relationship, there will be a blessed flow. God would have been preparing you both for the relationship that is within his will. Therefore he would have been preparing one of you (or both of you) to make the geographical sacrifices necessary to be together.

RULES FOR CROSS-DENOMINATIONAL DATING

RULE #1:

YOU MUST BOTH BELIEVE IN JESUS CHRIST AS LORD AND PERSONAL SAVIOR

This world is filled with all kinds of people, beliefs, and backgrounds which I think is amazing. I love diversity and learning about other cultures, traditions, and family heritage that differs from my own. When it comes to who I am going to marry and build a life with, however, that decision is not based on what is interesting or fascinating, but what the clearly written Word of God dictates. As modern-day Christians, it is extremely important that we know, understand, and submit our lives to God's written Word. The Word and will of God do not change because of societal norms and political pressures of dos and don'ts. God is the same yesterday, today, and forever.

For this reason, God has and always will desire Christians (believers in Christ Jesus as Lord AND Savior) to marry other Christians. This desire of God is clearly stated in 2 Corinthians 6:14-17 and threaded throughout both the Old and New Testaments. Yet, no matter how much I teach and preach this message, there are always arguments, not biblically based, but based on a woman's personal desire to be with a specific man. Her desire for self-satisfaction is stronger than her desire to please God. She also could be simply blinded to the truth because of strongholds in her mind, a belief system established from examining the lives of others who live outside of the will of God, a lack of inner faith based on her past failed relationships or lies that she has heard from others who also lack revelation knowledge.

When we do a full study of the word of God, we will find that the great God Jehovah was never okay with his followers marrying into idolatry or false god and pagan worship. God has always wanted born-again Christians to grow and multiply. This is not possible when his people marry others who do not believe in worshipping the Lord alone.

Contrary to popular belief, all paths do not lead to God. Some paths lead to false Gods or even a false Christ. The bible warns us about the increase in false teachers and prophets in the last days. Women desiring marriage must be vigilant, sober-minded, and make choices based on the Word, not on their flesh and emotions. It doesn't matter how good something sounds; it only matters if that belief is based on the Holy Scriptures.

A counterfeit spirit is a deceiving spirit, something appearing real but indeed fake and untrue. That is its purpose. To deceive you while making you believe that the lie being fed is the truth. Or perhaps the watered-down version of the truth is okay, as long as you believe in Christ, it's also okay to mix in other beliefs and religions. This is an extremely dangerous and flawed way of living. There is only ONE way to the Father and that is through Christ (John 14:6).

Being unequally yoked as defined by 2 Corinthians 6:14-17 speaks of being on the same page spiritually, being a born-again believer in Christ Jesus, but should also be considered in other areas of personal and corporate worship.

Key points to consider:

♡ Do you both believe that the 66 books of the Bible are God's Holy, complete, and infallible Word of truth?

♡ Do you both believe in worship through song, praise, and prayer?

♡ Do you both believe in holiness, consecration, and progressive sanctification?

♡ Do you both believe in worship, learning, and growing spiritually in the house of God (also called joining or partnering with a church/ministry)?

♡ Do you both believe in spiritual gifts and the baptism of the Holy Spirit?

♡ Do you both believe in modeling your lives after Christ?

♡ Do you both believe in tithing and sowing financially?

The foundation of both of your belief systems is so important in determining whether you both serve and worship the Lord and Savior Jesus Christ, or if you are not equally yoked at all. Remember, God is a God of order. He is not the author of confusion. He will not lead you to consider marrying a man that would cause spiritual confusion between you as a couple or in raising your future/current children.

Here are more scriptures that you can study to go deeper and gain a more robust understanding of how important it is to marry another truly born-again Christian who not only shares the same morals and values, but the same foundation of faith in Christ Jesus alone:

Deuteronomy 7:3

Ezra 9:2

1 Corinthians 10:20-21

Leviticus 18:1-5

Galatians 5:19-20

1 Corinthians 6:9-10

Exodus 34:13-17

Genesis 28:1

2 Timothy 3:5

Ephesians 5:3-11

2 John 1:9

1 John 4:1

Leviticus 19:19

Isaiah 52:11

James 4:4

1 Corinthians 10:14

DEFINITIONS

Idolatry

Worship, sacrifice, offering, prayer, praise, consulting, contacting, and/or placing a belief, faith, and hope in any being, entity (living or nonliving), source, or item other than the Lord God.

False god

Any human-created, man-concocted greater/higher power.

Counterfeit spirit

Any spirit other than the Holy Spirit that claims to provide power, human experiences, or insight into the supernatural realm.

False teaching

Lessons and teaching based on any addition to or subtraction from the 66 books (also known as the Canon) of the Holy Bible. This includes adding any other books that hold the same (or more) weight of significance as the Holy Bible or adding any other person or entity that holds the same (or more) weight of significance as Jesus Christ.

RULE #2:

FOLLOW THE PATH OF PEACE AND WISDOM

Now, let's say you both serve and worship Jesus Christ as Lord & Savior, but you just come from different denominations. I am always aggressively encouraging every believer to find a church home to be planted in and nourished by and to serve God's people. When someone gives me an excuse about something that happened at a specific church, I tell them to go to another one. The beauty of this generation is that there are all different types of churches and ministries to associate with. When you study how all the various denominations began, you will find that differences in the worship service, music played, or types of prayer does not mean that one denomination is completely wrong and another is completely correct. We are all doing our best to live for God and interpret scripture in a manner that glorifies the Father.

As long as the person you are considering entering into a relationship with believes and follows Jesus Christ as Lord and Savior and allows the Word of God contained in the Holy Scriptures to guide their lives, you should be able to find a happy medium between your differences of worship and service. In other words, your belief systems are the same, but your expression of those beliefs is different. This is the true definition of cross-denomination dating.

Keep in mind that in accordance with Ephesians Chapter 5, once you are married, the husband will officially become the spiritual covering of your home. If you deceive yourself into thinking that you can take the spiritual reins in your home and everything will work out perfectly, you will be in for a rude awakening. Many women have shared their personal journey through this type of deception. They end up married and miserable or divorced and regretful. These women knew in their hearts that there were significant spiritual differences between their own faith and that of the man they were interested in, but they were head over heels for him to the point of compromise.

Your denominational differences cannot be so vast as to create spiritual insecurity within your spirit and mind, bring confusion into either of your lives, or create unnecessary tension.

If you truly are torn and cannot tell if this relationship is literally a match made in heaven, that's when examining your peace and praying for wisdom will come in. The Lord will not keep you in the dark; he will give you as much wisdom as you need to make an informed and biblical decision. There are many diverse ways God speaks to each of us as individuals, but you can trust that he will speak to you in a manner that you can understand and move forward. Remember, he is not the author of confusion...that's satan.

When you think about your present belief system and how much God has taught you over the years, compared to where the man of God is in his walk with Christ, the wisdom of God should provide a clear (and quick) answer to the question of whether you are compatible or not.

Here's a real-life example. I was once building a new friendship with a young man who was a believer in Christ Jesus, but from a vastly different denomination than my own. I believe in and practice the baptism of the Holy Spirit with the evidence of praying in other tongues. I believe and practice all the Gifts of the Spirit. I believe in both having a personal prayer language where you pray personally to God in an unknown tongue, as well as corporate tongues which take place only in a group setting and require an interpretation. My new friend, however, did not believe in any of these things. There is nothing wrong with our differences, yet this belief is a major part of my lifestyle and walk with Christ which would have been compromised had I stayed in a relationship with him.

You see, not only did he disagree with my beliefs, but he publicly mocked my beliefs and invited others to also laugh and disagree with something as absurd as praying in tongues. Now to me, this belief is not just something I do that sounds funny. I was led to a ministry at a pivotal time in my life that not only taught intensely about the movement of the Holy Spirit but also practiced (with balance) the Gifts of the Spirit. I have witnessed and personally experienced miracles, signs, and wonders by way of these supernatural encounters. The baptism of the Holy Spirit and my personal praying in tongues made a huge difference in my sanctification journey with God. The Gifts of the Spirit are an unmatched expression of God's power and play a huge role in evangelism.

This belief system for me is not small and is certainly not laughable or something to be brushed off. It's major. How could I grow close to and give my heart to a man who completely disagrees and is not even open to the conversation? I couldn't. Our lives would be so out of balance. Let's say one of us got sick. I would want to pray for supernatural healing by the power of God, yet he doesn't believe in the gifts of healings. If we came across a friend or family member that was tormented by a demonic spirit, I would be ready to pray for deliverance and expect manifestation just as Christ had when he walked this earth. He would not believe in the gift of faith or spiritual deliverance and would be resigned that the person would need to figure it out with their human willpower or concede to mental illness and bondage.

In this situation, I didn't need to pray and ask God what to do about the friendship or if this man could possibly be the one. The wisdom of God cried out, loud and clear. Our spiritual differences were too vast, even though we were both born-again Christians.

THINK ABOUT THIS: If God has matured you to a certain place spiritually, why then would he want you to marry someone who is not on the same page as you? Why would God have led you to the right teachers, leaders, pastors, preachers, and godly examples, just so that you can place those things on the back burner for a relationship? No, no, no. If the Lord has raised you up in the spirit because of his will and plan for your life, he would have also raised your husband up in the spirit, giving him the same or similar revelations so that you two could join together and focus on putting 10,000 to flight (Deuteronomy 32:30), not on maneuvering through denominational differences and points of contention. What kind of peace will you have?

RULE #3:

COMPARE YOUR PERSONAL AND CORPORATE WORSHIP

A s discussed in Rule #12 you and your new man's life should fit together like a puzzle, flowing in harmony in every way. I am not talking about perfection, but I am talking about a blessed flow to your relationship. Therefore, even as you consider whether your different denominations will work well together, consider both your personal and corporate worship.

Look at each of your personal lifestyles of worship based on your denominational differences and be honest with yourself. The fear of marrying wrongly should outweigh the fear of extending your singleness. Let's say you're a woman who like me, prays daily, studies the Word of God for practical application daily, fasts and prays as you're led and operates regularly in what you believe is your God-given life's purpose. You attend church, submit to church leadership, listen to and honor your pastor, you tithe, sow and give into the ministry. You even serve in the house of God and look forward to doing the works of Christ daily.

Then you meet a man who prays here and there, studies the Word of God for answers only when he is in a bind, and doesn't know what his life's purpose is. He belongs to a ministry, but he doesn't believe in tithing or sowing financially into the church. He listens to other teachings of "spiritual" people and doesn't believe in the ministry of reconciliation (personal evangelism) but instead participates in what those other religions or philosophies have to offer.

When you go to visit his church, you feel extremely uncomfortable with the preaching and teaching presented. You don't feel as if it was biblically sound, but rather based on stirring up the emotions of the crowd. Or you didn't discern the Holy Spirit's presence at all in the service. When he visits your church, the service makes him uncomfortable and he thinks your pastor is being too deep or perhaps the message was for others, just not for him.

Minor denominational differences can make a huge difference in how you each spend your time and make decisions about your lives. There could be extreme differences such as what is acceptable attire both during church service and in your personal lives, as well the core teaching and beliefs can be on opposite ends of the spectrum (even though you both attend Christian ministries) and the level of ministry leadership involvement in your personal lives can be so extremely different that there is no way to make the relationship work without one person living in misery.

This is not God's will for either of you. The Lord wants you both to be in a happy and blessed relationship where you can flow spiritually and encourage each other to go higher with God. You should thrive in both your personal and corporate worship, as well as in your relationship.

Now, let's say you have minor differences, but the other person is more than willing to come on board and learn a new way of personal and corporate worship. Perhaps God has been giving that person inklings before you met that he wanted them to change or adjust their worship. There is a difference between taking a man at ground zero (meaning he has never been saved) and raising him up spiritually while you're dating him versus taking a man who already has a lifestyle of worship in motion, yet desires more from God and assisting him in going higher by introducing him to your world. The latter man is already in motion. You are not doing the Holy Spirit's job in bringing conviction, you are just the catalyst the Holy Spirit will use to open his eyes to another way of personal and corporate worship.

Or, if you turn the tables, let's say you have been led to have new spiritual experiences but are not sure where to start or go. When you meet this new man friend, he can open your eyes to new endeavors that are still in alignment with your ultimate beliefs. You will have much peace and excitement in learning more about the things of God. Your spirit will feel right at home when you visit his church. His words and teaching will minister deeply to your spirit. You may have a few questions but there will not be any confusion. When you both fit in easily with each other's worlds, this is a clear sign that although you have denominational differences, God can still do amazing things in your lives once the two become one.

RULES FOR ONLINE DATING

The following rules apply whether you meet someone on a dating app, website, social media message or inbox, or any other online source with capabilities of communicating and exchanging information with others.

RULE #1:

MAKE NO CONCESSIONS

Quite some time ago I had an online dating stint. It only lasted a few months, but it was just enough time for me to ignore all the red flags, throw my deal breakers in the toilet, break my celibacy walk and wind up with a broken heart. It was like a whirlwind of spiritual confusion, sexual sin, deep inner regret and emotional torment. It was baffling to me how quickly everything spiraled out of control. It was as if I was watching a bad romantic comedy...only it wasn't funny. I was celibate, living holy and spiritually strong...or so I thought.

It was in this season that I met what I still believe is the devil's best counterfeit of a potential husband: the good deacon. After seeing yet another relationship app commercial on TV, I decided to download a total of three apps to hedge my bets. One app was exclusively for black people, the other was expensive so I considered it "high-end" and the third was totally free, but I had seen two commercials for the app in the span of two weeks which was unheard of. To this day, I have never seen another TV commercial for this particular dating app and when I ask around, most people have never heard of it.

On this very quiet, peaceful Saturday afternoon, while my two-year old was napping upstairs, I opened the windows allowing the sun and cool fall breeze to pour into my living room. I snuggled into my comfy couch and got-to-swiping.

After a few hours, up pops this chocolate brown handsome man, striking up a conversation in my inbox. During this season of my life, I decided to be very kind during initial conversations with men but also ask bold questions up front, so as not to waste anyone's time, neither his nor mine. I found out quickly that not only was he saved (allegedly) but that he was also a deacon at this church.

What really impressed me the most in addition to our long and intense late-night conversations was his servitude. When I found out that he served every Wednesday night, taking care of the homeless with a ministry hosted by an organization not affiliated with his church, I was sure he was the type of man that I wanted in my life.

During one of our late-night conversations, he mentioned how he had been praying to God for his wife, and how I sounded like her. It was at that moment the devil had me. To know Sarita, the renowned author and life coach, is to know that I preach and teach very aggressively about how important it is to pray for your future husband. That means not only to pray for him as a request to God, but to intercede on his behalf, even before you meet. I also believe whole-heartedly that true men of God are prayerful while they are single. They don't become prayerful only after they get married. Therefore, a true man of God is praying for his future wife, just as single women are praying to God about their future husband. So to hear this man of God, this cute deacon who served the homeless with his free time tell me that not only was he praying for his wife (which I had never heard a single man every admit until after he was married) but that I sounded like her, was exactly what caused me to make unlimited concessions during this whirlwind relationship of deception.

The full story of what took place with the good deacon can be found in my book How to Heal a Broken Heart: Transition from Pain to Peace. Here I will summarize exactly what the deception was and the outcome. It was true that he was an ordained deacon and had a servant's heart. However, he was also a weed smoking, cursing, sex having, low-key homosexual tendency having, spiritually confused man of God. These issues became evident over the course of our relationship. Unfortunately, he had already talked me out of my panties by the time all the layers of the onion were pulled back.

This is why it is very important not to make any concessions when you meet someone online. Phone conversations are very intimate, even though you are not together in person. Once you have each other's undivided attention, words are exchanged, hearts and minds are open and it's easy to become vulnerable and transparent early on. However, just like any other relationship, you must allow time to confirm everything that he is saying and allow him to prove that he is the man he is presenting to you.

Now here's the game. Men who operate with a counterfeit, demonic spirit will read your online profile and say things that line up with what you say you want from and desire in a man, just to get close to you. Remember, the devil's job is to break you. He wants to drive you far away from God and chip away at your faith. The devil wants you to believe that there is no one who will love you the way you truly desire to be loved, there is no man who is filled with and led by God's Spirit at the level you need, that your standards are too high and you're asking for too much.

Remember a counterfeit is supposed to look like the real thing. Online dating has provided an additional avenue for counterfeits to run rampant and tear through the hearts of women. That's why it's so important to make no concessions.

The concessions I made with the deacon included overlooking the lack of fruitfulness in his life because I was so enthralled with his service of God's people. He lived with his mom but had an amazing story of how he ended up in that situation that made him appear as if he was coming to her (and his 10 nieces and nephew's) rescue. He had just started out at a new job, at the bottom of the totem pole, yet he was a middle-aged man. His lifestyle choices of smoking weed, getting drunk, and cursing, were things I thought I was supposed to be patient about and pray him through. Finally, when it came to studying and teaching scripture, I realized his understanding was flawed when he focused his study on one specific book of the Bible yet disregarded the other 65 canons. These were all very blatant signs that God was not a part of this connection, but I disregarded my discernment and tried to pray about everything. I made a big mistake.

Now, had we met in person initially, I would have been aware of many of these issues earlier on. Those lengthy late-night conversations had my mind and heart wide open. He was such a smooth-talking man, truly the perfect deception that caused me to backslide.

I don't want this to happen to you. Be crystal clear about what you want. Be uncompromising on those things you consider deal breakers. After all, they are deal breakers for a reason. Don't get so caught up in all the right words he may say because after all, he read your profile. There are many men online that are preying on desperate Christian women. I know, you don't consider yourself desperate. I didn't consider myself desperate either, but I found out one day (quite by accident) that this was exactly how he saw ANY woman that he met online. He saw us as desperate, sad, and lonely. I was far from any of those things, I was simply exploring another avenue to meet men. There were no negative emotions driving me to get online, it was simply exploration and trying something new. When I got offline after that season, I never went back to those waters again.

The reason why women are catfished so easily is because of those intimate conversations. Words are extremely powerful. Part of guarding your heart is protecting your ears from words that sound as sweet as honey but will lead you into a trap of deception.

Of course, I am not saying that all men online are trifling. I am saying, be careful and don't make any concessions just because you met them online.

RULE #2:

STAY IN THE PRESENCE OF GOD

Never leave the presence of God to be found by or enter into a relationship with a man. Whether you meet on or offline you should never have to place your personal spiritual convictions to the side to appease a man you are interested in. Likewise, you must remain diligent in your prayer and study time, attending worship services, serving within the Body of Christ, etc., even as you explore new opportunities to meet men.

The advice given to most single women in this generation is to "put yourself out there" more so that you can meet a man. But if putting yourself out there includes spending more time on dating websites/apps than you do with the things of God, you have prioritized finding a man over your personal relationship with God.

Staying in the presence of God is very important so that

your discernment will remain sharp, and you can hear from the Lord concerning the relationship. Whether he gives you warning signs about the man or confirmation that this is the ordained relationship he has for you, you must keep your spirit sensitive.

Many of the conversations I have had with women who have jumped into online dating are not making the move because they have prayed and heard from God. Rather, they are tired of waiting and caught up in the promises of simplicity finding love online versus traditionally. The advertisements for online dating look amazing, as they should. A good marketing campaign is very intriguing. So intriguing and enticing is the thought of quickly and easily sorting through the weeds and hand selecting the perfect match, women have decided not to wait on the Lord any longer, but to take matters into their own hands. When you make choices and move ahead of God or outside of God's leadership and timing, you have effectively decided to leave his presence to make a relationship happen by your own strength.

When you meet a man online, it can be tricky not to fall for the man you see on paper, literally. Falling for the man on paper is what has caused many women (including myself) to let their guards down too early and tip toe outside of the presence of God for the sake of the relationship. The online and over the phone persona of the deacon laid the foundation for the me to break rule #1 above, which in turn led me outside of the presence of God while in a relationship with him.

While dating him I drank alcohol, broke my celibacy walk, and started questioning the foundation of my faith, all under his influence. It's true that this could have taken place with a man I met in person, but the combination of his online persona, the late night very intimate conversations and his initial presentation as this highly spiritual and knowledge-able ordained minister led me further from God, instead of closer to him. He didn't encourage me towards godliness, but instead brought about confusion and a new season of backsliding.

To make this clearer, it felt as though when I was with him (physically in his presence), I was not near God at that moment. I had to ignore my discernment and do those things that made me completely uncomfortable because I knew better, yet I wanted to make him happy. It's amazing how much a woman will give of herself and her personal identity in order to land or hold onto the possibility of a rela-tionship that leads to marriage.

God is a jealous God. He has warned us time and time again in the Holy Scriptures to never place anything or any person before him. He also wants us to live balanced lives (Proverbs 11:1). We can rest assured that when we seek God as priority, we will never lose a man or miss out on our dream marriage as long as we keep him and the kingdom first.

RULE #3:

FOLLOW THE PROCESS

The process of getting to know a man, hearing from God about the relationship, date, court and then marry is a blessed and necessary progression of any relationship. First Corinthians 14:40 says that God does all things decently and in order. When you meet a potential love interest online versus in person, it can be tempting to rush ahead and skip steps in the process. This is because online you have more access to details of that person's shared life. While not every man you meet is regularly posting on social media, they all will have some form of presence online. After all, that's how you met. The picture-perfect man appears on their profile page. They are going to put their best foot forward. He will present an image of a together, smart and successful man of God. Yet in real life, beneath the surface lies much more than online appearances present.

As I previously stated, because the online persona is so beautiful, it can be easy to let your guard down and move a bit faster in the dating and relationship process. I have found that men will maintain the same pace of relationship progression, no matter how they meet a woman, but women are the opposite. Because you spend time not only reading his online profile but digging deeper into his entire online activity (as much as you can find) you tend to rush to judgment, let your guards down, and move too fast too quickly.

Once you view his story, check out how he communicates with others, look through all his pictures (and everything in the background of those photos), research his other online profiles across various sites and apps, if everything seems on the up and up, you are full speed ahead and "off to the races" so to speak. Of course, I am not saying that every woman goes through this type of online research in a new prospect, but most do.

You feel like you know him a little better, not because of your interaction with him, but simply because of the amount of research you have done. He, on the other hand, has not done half of the research into you as you have into him. He is going with the flow, following the process, and getting to know you in real life.

There are no blanket statements here...but I am sure you can relate. You have done your fair share of online research into a man you were truly interested in (even if you didn't meet online), in hopes of learning more about him in between the phone conversations or video meetings and dates.

Men who prey on women that are online searching for love understand that women will rush the process when they meet what appears to be the perfect man online. This is how women end up being scammed by perpetrators they have only met and interacted with via technology. The scammers know that all they need to do is present a perfect online image and say just the right words to a certain type of woman and she will trust him totally, even before she meets him in person or in a video call.

Following the process of friendship building, getting to know each other, deciding on a mutually exclusive relationship with each other, and progressing towards courtship, then marriage, is extremely important whether you meet online or offline. Yet again, the ease of access to what may be a plethora of information makes it easier to skip a few steps and jump ahead if you think you are privy to the key information you need to know in order to move forward emotionally.

It's imperative to follow the process, allowing the relationship to take a natural progression. During the dating and relationship process, you will find out if the words he speaks to you virtually line up with his actual life. You will move beyond talking on the phone or responding to a text to meeting in person, spending quality time in each other's presence. You will have the opportunity to examine the fruit of his life, exercise your discernment, hear from God, and truly understand the type of man he is.

Allow your relationship to experience gradual, progressive forward movement at a blessed pace as you are led by the Holy Spirit. The Holy Spirit wants to speak, teach, and reveal information to you about the man, yourself, and the relationship throughout the process.

When it comes to getting to know the man, you want to explore how he handles all sorts of situations, which can only be viewed over the course of time. There are also more lessons to learn about yourself such as truly understanding what type of personality, interactions, and communications bring out the best in you. The Lord will also reveal more of himself during the relationship, such as how to access wisdom from the Holy Spirit while engaging with one another.

You must give God some time to bring forth confirmation and reveal all things that may lie ahead for your both, the good and the bad. Rushing through this process of learning and progression is never a good idea.

I am not saying that you need to be friends for three years, engaged for five years and then finally roll around to marriage. I believe we live in an age of supernatural marriage, in which God is connecting God-fearing couples that will have an accelerated dating and courtship so they can get married, raise a family, and glorify God in their marriage quickly. Even in this case, however, your relationship should still progress in a manner that makes sense. Wisdom, discretion, and common sense are still in the mix of your decision-making. In other words, you will still have the opportunity to explore each other's lives offline as well as online. There will still be time to witness his responses and actions in varied situations. You will still have the opportunity to meet each other's friends and families in person. You will also have the chance to understand each other's beliefs and plans for raising a new family. Relationship development will simply take place at a faster pace, at which you will both find peace and grace throughout the process.

ABOUT THE AUTHOR

Sarita A. Foxworth is a Bible Teacher, Author & Retreat Host for single Christian women. Her life's mission is teaching how to date smarter, grow in faith, and operate in high levels of purpose and calling. She does this through her books, coaching programs, events, and luxury retreats.

In 2010 Sarita began serving and teaching women at her home Bible study groups focusing on health, beauty, love, and life's purpose. The group grew over the next four years and testimonies poured in. Women were getting married, growing in their confidence and understanding of who they were as women, and stepping into their life's purpose and calling.

To increase her skillset in helping women spiritually, personally, and professionally she attended The Coaching and Positive Psychology Institute in 2014, receiving a certification as a Personal and Executive Life Coach. Shortly after graduation, she started her Christian life coaching business, offering personal coaching programs, luxury retreats, and self-publishing programs for new authors.

Since then, she launched a worldwide ministry of fasting and prayer and has written over twelve books curated for single Christian women and new authors. She also teaches regular Bible studies to help women practically apply the truth of God's Word to daily living.

Sarita actively works to connect like-minded women of faith and create a responsive community of support and love while challenging women to make a significant impact in this generation to the glory of God. She invites you to join this beautiful community by subscribing to her Youtube page or following her Instagram posts and conversations. It would be her honor to serve as your mentor and life coach. You can also connect with Sarita by signing up on her email list at www.SaritaFoxworth.com.

NEXT STEPS

CONNECT WITH ME

This book was powerful, wasn't it! The Holy Spirit was integral to the writing process. I'd LOVE to hear how it's blessed your life! Please share your review on Amazon.com. You can also share a cute picture of this book with your audience and tag me on Instagram (@Sarita.foxworth), so I can find it!

The best way to connect with me is by joining my email list at www.SaritaFoxworth.com. I send out evening devotionals, weekly encouragement and have a private "ask Sarita" email series to engage with real women like you regularly.

Want to meet me at a live event, prayer meeting, or retreat? Once you're on the email list, you will be the first to know upcoming event details and get first access invitations to virtual and live events.

GO DEEPER

If you have been struggling with doubt and fear concerning your singleness or the season of waiting, go to my Youtube page (Sarita A. Foxworth) and check out a Bible study series I created called: God Wants You Married. This series includes a Bible study notes download with over 30 faith-inducing scriptures about kingdom marriage.

SCAN ME

Watch the Bible study series called: God Wants You Married.

BOOK SHOP

All books are available worldwide for purchase directly from the Love & Miracles Book Boutique. Whether you need help hearing from God in prayer, understanding your pro-phetic anointing, or learning and loving the woman you, there is a book that will greatly bless your life!

You can also purchase a group book order inclusive of bulk discount pricing from the

L & M Publishing website www.lmpublishing.co. There are also beautiful gifts to choose from that will wow your audience!

Made in the USA
Monee, IL
23 April 2025

16284357R00129